Alpine Trials & Rallies

Martin Pfundner

in co-operation with Count Hans Christoph Seherr-Thoss and Andrew Swann

VELOCE PUBLISHING
THE PUBLISHER OF FINE AUTOMOTIVE BOOKS

Also from Veloce Publishing -

SpeedPro Series
4-Cylinder Engine - How to Blueprint & Build a Short Block for High Performance by Des Hammill
Alfa Romeo Twin Cam Engines - How to Power Tune by Jim Kartalamakis
BMC 998cc A-Series Engine - How to Power Tune by Des Hammill
BMC/Rover 1275cc A-Series Engine - How to Power Tune by Des Hammill
Camshafts - How to Choose & Time them for Maximum Power by Des Hammill
Cylinder Heads - How to Build, Modify & Power Tune Updated & Revised Edition by Peter Burgess
Distributor-type Ignition Systems - How to Build & Power Tune by Des Hammill
Fast Road Car - How to Plan and Build New Edition by Daniel Stapleton
Ford SOHC 'Pinto' & Sierra Cosworth DOHC Engines - How to Power Tune Updated & Enlarged Editionby Des Hammill
Ford V8 - How to Power Tune Small Block Engines by Des Hammill
Harley-Davidson Evolution Engines - How to Build & Power Tune by Des Hammill
Holley Carburetors - How to Build & Power Tune New Edition by Des Hammill
Jaguar XK Engines - How to Power Tune New Edition by Des Hammill
MG Midget & Austin-Healey Sprite - How to Power Tune Updated Edition by Daniel Stapleton
MGB 4-Cylinder Engine - How to Power Tune by Peter Burgess
MGB - How to Give your MGB V8 Power Updated & Revised Edition by Roger Williams
MGB, MGC & MGB V8 - How to Improve by Roger Williams
Mini Engines - How to Power Tune on a Small Budget 2nd Edition by Des Hammill
Motorsport - Getting Started in by SS Collins
Nitrous Oxide by Trevor Langfield
Rover V8 Engines - How to Power Tune by Des Hammill
Sportscar/Kitcar Suspension & Brakes - How to Build & Modify Enlarged & Updated 2nd Edition by Des Hammill
SU Carburettors - How to Build & Modify for High Performance by Des Hammill
Suzuki 4WD by John Richardson
Tiger Avon Sportscar - How to Build Your Own Updated & Revised 2nd Edition by Jim Dudley
TR2, 3 & TR4 - How to Improve by Roger Williams
TR5, 250 & TR6 - How to Improve by Roger Williams
V8 Engine - How to Build a Short Block for High Performance by Des Hammill
Volkswagen Beetle Suspension, Brakes & Chassis - How to Modify for High Performance by James Hale
Volkswagen Bus Suspension, Brakes & Chassis - How to Modify for High Performance by James Hale
Weber DCOE, & Dellorto DHLA Carburetors - How to Build & Power Tune 3rd Edition by Des Hammill

Those were the days ... Series
Alpine Rallies by Martin Pfundner
Austerity Motoring by Malcolm Bobbitt
Brighton National Speed Trials by Tony Gardiner
British Police Cars by Nick Walker
Crystal Palace by Sam Collins
Dune Buggy Phenomenon by James Hale
Dune Buggy Phenomenon Volume 2 by James Hale
Motor Racing at Brands Hatch in the Seventies by Chas Parker
Motor Racing at Goodwood in the Sixties by Tony Gardiner
Three Wheelers by Malcolm Bobbitt

Enthusiast's Restoration Manual Series
Citroen 2CV, How to Restore by Lindsay Porter
Classic Car Body Work, How to Restore by Martin Thaddeus
Classic Cars, How to Paint by Martin Thaddeus
Reliant Regal, How to Restore by Elvis Payne
Triumph TR2/3/3A, How to Restore by Roger Williams
Triumph TR4/4A, How to Restore by Roger Williams
Triumph TR5/250 & 6, How to Restore by Roger Williams
Triumph TR7/8, How to Restore by Roger Williams
Volkswagen Beetle, How to Restore by Jim Tyler

Essential Buyer's Guide Series
Alfa GT Buyer's Guide by Keith Booker
Alfa Romeo Spider by Keith Booker
Jaguar E-Type Buyer's Guide
Porsche 928 Buyer's Guide by David Hemmings
VW Beetle Buyer's Guide by Richard Copping & Ken Czervenka
VW Bus Buyer's Guide by Richard Copping & Ken Czervenka

Auto-Graphics Series
Fiat & Abarth by Andrea & David Sparrow
Jaguar MkII by Andrea & David Sparrow
Lambretta LI by Andrea & David Sparrow

General
AC Two-litre Saloons & Buckland Sportscars by Leo Archibald
Alfa Romeo Giulia Coupe GT & GTA by John Tipler
Alfa Tipo 33 by Ed McDonough
Anatomy of the Works Minis by Brian Moylan
Armstrong-Siddeley by Bill Smith
Autodrome by Sam Collins & Gavin Ireland
Automotive A-Z, Lane's Dictionary of Automotive Terms by Keith Lane
Automotive Mascots by David Kay & Lynda Springate
Bentley Continental, Corniche and Azure by Martin Bennett
BMC Competitions Department Secrets by Stuart Turner, Marcus Chambers & Peter Browning
BMW 5-Series by Marc Cranswick
BMW Z-Cars by James Taylor
British 250cc Racing Motorcycles by Chris Pereira
British Cars, The Complete Catalogue of, 1895-1975 by Culshaw & Horrobin
Bugatti Type 40 by Barrie Price
Bugatti 46/50 Updated Edition by Barrie Price

Bugatti 57 2nd Edition by Barrie Price
Caravans, The Illustrated History 1919-1959 by Andrew Jenkinson
Caravans, The Illustrated History from 1960 by Andrew Jenkinson
Chrysler 300 - America's Most Powerful Car 2nd Edition by Robert Ackerson
Citroen DS by Malcolm Bobbitt
Cobra - The Real Thing! by Trevor Legate
Cortina - Ford's Bestseller by Graham Robson
Coventry Climax Racing Engines by Des Hammill
Daimler SP250 'Dart' by Brian Long
Datsun 240, 260 & 280Z by Brian Long
Dune Buggy Files by James Hale
Dune Buggy Handbook by James Hale
Fiat & Abarth 124 Spider & Coupe by John Tipler
Fiat & Abarth 500 & 600 2nd edition by Malcolm Bobbitt
Ford F100/F150 Pick-up 1948-1996 by Robert Ackerson
Ford F150 1997-2005 by Robert Ackerson
Ford GT40 by Trevor Legate
Ford Model Y by Sam Roberts
Funky Mopeds by Richard Skelton
Honda NSX by Brian Long
Jaguar, The Rise of by Barrie Price
Jaguar XJ-S by Brian Long
Jeep CJ by Robert Ackerson
Jeep Wrangler by Robert Ackerson
Karmann-Ghia Coupe & Convertible by Malcolm Bobbitt
Land Rover, The Half-Ton Military by Mark Cook
Lea-Francis Story, The by Barrie Price
Lexus Story, The by Brian Long
Lola - The Illustrated History (1957-1977) by John Starkey
Lola - All The Sports Racing & Single-Seater Racing Cars 1978-1997 by John Starkey
Lola T70 - The Racing History & Individual Chassis Record 3rd Edition by John Starkey
Lotus 49 by Michael Oliver
Marketing Mobiles, The Wonderful Wacky World of, by James Hale
Mazda MX-5/Miata 1.6 Enthusiast's Workshop Manual by Rod Grainger & Pete Shoemark
Mazda MX-5/Miata 1.8 Enthusiast's Workshop Manual by Rod Grainger & Pete Shoemark
Mazda MX-5 (& Eunos Roadster) - The World's Favourite Sportscar by Brian Long
Mazda MX-5 Miata Roadster by Brian Long
MGA by John Price Williams
MGB & MGB GT - Expert Guide (Auto-Doc Series) by Roger Williams
Micro Caravans by Andrew Jenkinson
Mini Cooper - The Real Thing! by John Tipler
Mitsubishi Lancer Evo by Brian Long
Motor Racing Reflections by Anthony Carter
Motorhomes, The Illustrated History by Andrew Jenkinson
Motorsport in colour, 1950s by Martyn Wainwright
MR2 - Toyota's Mid-engined Sports Car by Brian Long
Nissan 300ZX & 350Z - The Z-Car Story by Brian Long
Pass the Theory and Practical Driving Tests by Clive Gibson & Gavin Hoole
Pontiac Firebird by Marc Cranswick
Porsche Boxster by Brian Long
Porsche 356 by Brian Long
Porsche 911 Carrera - The Last of the Evolution by Tony Corlett
Porsche 911R, RS & RSR, 4th Edition by John Starkey
Porsche 911 - The Definitive History 1963-1971 by Brian Long
Porsche 911 - The Definitive History 1971-1977 by Brian Long
Porsche 911 - The Definitive History 1977-1987 by Brian Long
Porsche 911 - The Definitive History 1987-1997 by Brian Long
Porsche 911 - The Definitive History 1997-2004 by Brian Long
Porsche 911SC The Essential Companion by Adrian Streather
Porsche 914 & 914-6 by Brian Long
Porsche 924 by Brian Long
Porsche 993 'King of Porsche' - The Essential Companion by Adrian Streather
Porsche 944 by Brian Long
RAC Rally Action! by Tony Gardiner
Rolls-Royce Silver Shadow/Bentley T Series Corniche & Camargue Revised & Enlarged Edition by Malcolm Bobbitt
Rolls-Royce Silver Spirit, Silver Spur & Bentley Mulsanne 2nd Edition by Malcolm Bobbitt
Rolls-Royce Silver Wraith, Dawn & Cloud/Bentley MkVI, R & S Series by Martyn Nutland
RX-7 - Mazda's Rotary Engine Sportscar (updated & revised new edition) by Brian Long
Singer Story: Cars, Commercial Vehicles, Bicycles & Motorcycles by Kevin Atkinson
Subaru Impreza by Brian Long
Taxi! The Story of the London Taxicab by Malcolm Bobbitt
Triumph Motorcycles & the Meriden Factory by Hughie Hancox
Triumph Speed Twin & Thunderbird Bible by Harry Woolridge
Triumph Tiger Cub Bible by Mike Estall
Triumph Trophy Bible by Harry Woolridge
Triumph TR6 by William Kimberley
Turner's Triumphs, Edward Turner & his Triumph Motorcycles by Jeff Clew
Velocette Motorcycles - MSS to Thruxton Updated & Revised Edition by Rod Burris
Volkswagen Bus or Van to Camper, How to Convert by Lindsay Porter
Volkswagens of the World by Simon Glen
VW Beetle Cabriolet by Malcolm Bobbitt
VW Beetle - The Car of the 20th Century by Richard Copping
VW Bus, Camper, Van, Pickup by Malcolm Bobbitt
VW - The air-cooled era by Richard Copping
Works Rally Mechanic by Brian Moylan

First published in 2005 by Veloce Publishing Limited, 33 Trinity Street, Dorchester DT1 1TT, England. Fax 01305 268864/e-mail info@veloce.co.uk/web www.veloce.co.uk or www.velocebooks.com
ISBN 1-904788-95-5/UPC 36847-00395-1
British Library Cataloguing in Publication Data - A catalogue record for this book is available from the British Library. Typesetting, design and page make-up all by Veloce Publishing Ltd on Apple Mac. Printed in Spain by Grafo.

Contents

Illustration credits

The author wishes to acknowledge and thank the following for providing photographs and other illustrations. Unfortunately, despite all efforts, it has not been possible to identify the original sources of all the pictures.

Alfa Romeo, Centro di documentazione storica, Milano
Allgemeine Automobil Zeitung (AAZ), Vienna
Hero Alting Archive, Osnabrück
ARBÖ, Vienna
Austro Classic, Wolfgang Buchta, Kierling
Auto Jahr, Lausanne
Autorevue, Vienna
Audi AG (Auto-Union Archive), Ingolstadt
Odette Avril, Noirmoutier en l'Ile
BMW Archive Mobile Tradition, Munich
British Leyland/Jaguar, Coventry
Adriano Cimarosti, Frauenkappelen
Angus Cundey, London
DaimlerChrysler Classic Medien - und Konzernarchiv, Stuttgart

Peter Denzel (Wolfgang Denzel AG), Vienna
Guy Griffiths Collection, Brighton
Count Heinrich von der Mühle, Leonberg Castle
ÖAMTC, Vienna
Austrian National Library, Vienna
Martin Pfundner, Archive, Vienna
Porsche Archive, Stuttgart
Count Seherr-Thoss Automobile Archive, Munich
Dipl-Ing Rainer Simons, Munich
Andrew Swann (Archive), Bromsgrove, Worcestershire
Technical Museum, Vienna
Bernhard Völker, Stuttgart
Michael Wright, Budleigh Salterton, Devon
Michael Zappe, Vienna

in association with
The Michael Sedgwick Trust

This work is published with the assistance of the Michael Sedgwick Trust. Founded in memory of the famous motoring researcher and author Michael Sedgwick (1926-1983), the Trust is a registered charity to encourage new research and the recording of motoring history. Suggestions for future projects, and donations, should be sent to the Honorary Secretary of the Michael Sedgwick Trust, c/o the John Montagu Building, Beaulieu, Hampshire, SO42 7ZN, England.

Foreword

In the beginning there was just one Alpine Trial, organized by the Imperial Royal Austrian Automobile Club between 1910 and 1914. As the most arduous test for touring cars, and the ultimate adventure for the drivers, it became a legend. Thanks to Rolls-Royce publicity following the company's resounding success in 1913, this legend spread well beyond the confines of Central Europe.

The original Alpine Trial did not survive World War I for the simple reason that the Habsburg Monarchy was torn apart. In the twenties and thirties other countries claimed their share in the prestigious name, and soon there were Alpine Trials and Rallies galore – Austrian, French, German, Hungarian, Italian, Swiss, and Yugoslav. The crowning event was, however, the International Alpine Trials of 1928 to 1936, organized jointly by up to seven National Automobile Clubs. Confusion reigned, and the resulting maze of well over a hundred Alpine Trials and Rallies has been an enigma to laymen and experts alike ever since.

This book attempts to disentangle the highly confusing scene by providing a road map through the labyrinth of Alpine Trials and Rallies.

As far as I am aware this is the first such attempt. Alpine Trials or Rallies, and the success stories of particular makes are mentioned in many books, but no overall history has ever been recorded. My research, therefore, had to concentrate on the motoring magazines, daily newspapers, and original results lists of yesteryear, particularly *Allgemeine Automobil Zeitung* (Vienna), *Auto Italiana* (Milan), *Automobil Revue* (Berne), *Automobile Year* (Lausanne), *Autorevue* (Vienna), *Auto-Touring* (Vienna), *L'Equipe* (Paris), *Marseille-Auto, Motor und Sport* (Stuttgart), *The Autocar* (London), and *The Motor* (London).

In the preparation of this work I have had a great number of friendly helpers, and my thanks are due to all of them. However, I must single out two because their flow of contributions exceeded all my expectations. I have profited from the immense knowledge of an age-old friend in Munich, Count Hans Christoph von Seherr-Thoss, a prominent member of the FIA's Commission Historique Internationale. The other is Andrew Swann in England, a great collector of Alpine

HJ Aldington, in his Frazer Nash, won a Glacier Cup in the 1932 International Alpine Trial. Painting by Michael Wright. Car and painting are now owned by Angus Cundey.

relics. These, and all the information drawn from them, have made Andrew an outstanding expert on the history of the International Alpine Trials and French Alpine Rallies.

When the original Alpine Trial was first run, its purpose was to breed touring cars fit for the Alps – and mountains in general. Even in 1952, Sunbeam-Talbot proudly declared its cars 'Bred in the Alps'. For more than six decades the Alpine

The Opel of Franz Traiser enters the Parc Fermé for scrutineering
(International Alpine 1934).

contributed to the development of the motor car. The memory
of these great events is still alive, and each year in Austria,
Switzerland and France historic or nostalgic Alpine Rallies
are organized for well-preserved and restored motor cars of
yesteryear.

Martin Pfundner
Vienna

Paul von Guilleaume in his Adler Trumpf heading for the top of the
Stelvio (International Alpine 1934).

Prelude – The Stelvio 1898

Although motor sport had existed in a variety of forms since the 1894 Paris-Rouen event, which was held on the good roads in the plains of Northern France, tackling an Alpine mountain pass with a fragile and underpowered early motor car was quite another matter. We owe the first written account of such an undertaking to Pierre Souvestre, a French homme de lettres. He relates how, in 1895, le Comte Cognard in a Peugeot Quadricycle mastered the St Gotthard Pass in Switzerland. Although this was a remarkable achievement, it wasn't actually as part of a motoring competition. The first speed hill climb in history only happened two years later at La Turbie in the mountainous hinterland of the French Riviera, uphill from Nice and Monte Carlo. Fastest was a 15hp De Dion Steam Car driven by 'Pary', pseudonym of a certain André Michelin.

But what was a short speed hill climb compared with conquering the Alps? From 27th until 29th August 1898, the Austrian Touring Club organized a bicycle race through South Tyrol and permitted motor cars to compete alongside the cyclists. The 'Automobile Run Through South Tyrol' started in Trafoi at the famous Stelvio Pass, then still called Stilfser Joch, and competitors were to proceed to Cortina d'Ampezzo before turning west to arrive at the finish in Bozen (Bolzano), a total distance of 465.6 kilometres, or 289.2 miles. Five cars were entered, but there were two non-starters, one of whom was Emil Jellinek whose new Daimler could not be delivered in time. His daughter's first name – Mercedes – was soon to become the brand name for all Daimler cars.

Only three cars actually started in this first ever motor race in the Austro-Hungarian Monarchy, at the same time the very first road race over majestic mountain passes in the world. Dr Eduard Suchanek, President of the Austrian Touring Club, was acting as Steward of the Meeting and, as such, rode in one of the competing cars, the 4hp Daimler of Herr Eduard Bierenz. In his report Suchanek wrote that Gottlieb Daimler, despite his advanced age, did not shy from many hours of strenuous railway travel from Switzerland, arriving in Bozen (Bolzano) by the morning train. His motor car with the new magneto-electric ignition had also been transported there by rail.

Although Gottlieb Daimler participated in the event as an observer, two of his cars had been entered by his agents for Austria, a 4hp Daimler for Eduard Bierenz and a 6hp one for Adalbert Hermann. Daimler saw to it that nothing was left to chance, however, and both cars were chauffeured by the best driving mechanics from the Cannstatt works, Wilhelm Werner in the Bierenz car, and Wilhelm Bauer in the one entered by Hermann.

Competition came from Baron Theodor Liebieg in his 7hp Benz. Although seriously unwell and soon to retire, Liebieg still managed to show his driving skill on the Stelvio road, as Suchanek remembered: "After having covered the first hairpin bends at a comparatively moderate pace, this was soon increased to a tremendous racing speed on the straight downhill road beyond the fortress of Hommagoi. The reason was that Baron Liebieg, together with Director Jellinek, certainly the senior and most experienced Austrian motorist, was coming in sight. He was cornering with astounding driving skill as he was taking the hairpin bends above us. The speed of this wild chase must have been at least forty kilometres per hour (25mph) ..." which rendered conversation from car to car totally impossible, according to Eduard Suchanek's recollection.

Studying the old newspaper reports of slipping or torn leather drive belts of the Daimler transmission one begins to appreciate the monumental undertaking of racing across high mountain passes in those days. To cite Suchanek again: "At Untermais, a suburb of Meran [Merano] we had to make a ten minute stop to fix the seam of the 4th speed drive belt which had come undone some 15 kilometres before. As Werner, the mechanic, still believed Baron Liebieg to be in hot pursuit he had made only a makeshift repair, with dire consequences. After another 8 kilometres towards Bozen the somewhat worn-out drive belt broke anew, and into numerous pieces ..."

The Hermann Daimler suffered an upset of a different kind as described in the cable report of *Neue Freie Presse*, Vienna's leading daily: "Meran, 29th August. Near Schlanders, the motor car of Herr Adalbert Hermann collided with a coach from Bozen, the passengers of which were English ladies. Only the shaft of the carriage was broken, without any other damage.

The first ever race across the Alps was the 'Automobile Run through South Tyrol' of 1898, which was started at Trafoi at the Stelvio, with the Trafoi Hotel in the background. Seen here are the three participants: Adalbert Hermann/Wilhelm Bauer (6hp Daimler, no. 15, the winner), Baron Theodor von Liebieg (7hp Benz, no. 16, retired), and Josef Eduard Bierenz/Wilhelm Werner (4hp Daimler, no. 14, second).

Hermann's passenger Dr Christomanos offered bail which allowed the motor to continue the race."

Indeed, Britons male or female were always attracted by the Alps, long before the advent of proper Alpine Trials. In the end both Daimlers made it to the finish, the Hermann 6hp with Wilhelm Bauer at the wheel winning from the 4hp Bierenz car driven by Wilhelm Werner.

The Dolomites also taught Gottlieb Daimler an important technical lesson. From then on Daimler cars featured chain drive, and the belt-driven model was discontinued. Of the two drivers, Wilhelm Bauer was later killed in the 1900 La Turbie Hill Climb, whilst Wilhelm Werner became personal chauffeur of the German Emperor Wilhelm II, with the grandiose title of "Kaiserlicher Oberwagenführer".

The 1898 Automobile Run through South Tyrol was an important event in the history of motor sport, it was a race across the Alps, a pure speed event fashioned after the races in France, and should not, therefore, be considered a direct forerunner of the 'Alpenfahrt'. The latter made its name as a reliability trial, a pattern of motor sport that had its origins in Great Britain. In 1900 the Automobile Club of Great Britain and Ireland organized the 1000 Mile Trial as an alternative to the French-style city-to-city races that conflicted with the prevailing speed limits in the British Isles.

The quintessential difference between the French speed events – where one driver competed directly against the other – and this new type of competition was striking. In the Reliability Trial, the organizers formulated certain tasks or conditions which the driver had to meet or fulfil. Any deviation caused penalty points. Hence, the participant competed against the organizers, and could claim a first class award for meeting all the set conditions, or an inferior award if there were deviations in his performance. Such trials flourished in Britain, but across the Channel this alternative concept of motor sport remained almost unnoticed. To bring the new idea to the Continent was the great achievement of a Bavarian painter, Hubert von Herkomer. He went to England as a boy, worked as an illustrator for *The Graphic*, and then established himself as a portraitist, very much à la mode in late Victorian and Edwardian days. Once a year, however, he returned Bavaria for his holidays. There, in 1903, he came into contact with the President of the Bayerische Automobil Club, and the conversation turned to the Reliability Trials so popular in Britain. Herkomer offered to donate a Silver Challenge Trophy, plus a free portrait of the outright winner.

Between 1905 and 1907, the Herkomer Trials was established as the supreme reliability test for Touring Cars on the Continent of Europe. One of the reasons for its success was the active participation of the German Emperor's brother, Prince Henry of Prussia, which lent tremendous prestige to the event and to reliability trials in general. When the series of three Herkomer Trials came to an end in 1907, they were succeeded by the three Prinz Heinrich-Fahrten, of 1908 to 1910. Competing for a Silver Challenge Trophy donated by Prince Henry, the motor industry improved the Touring Car breed enormously. Germany can take credit for firmly establishing the Trial on the Continent.

The first Alpine Trials
1910-1914

The next club to keep the Trials flag flying was the Austrian Automobile Club. Since 1906 the club had staged an annual voiturette trial of minor importance. For 1910 this was upgraded to become the first Alpenfahrt, or Alpine Trial. Starting only a fortnight after the last proper Prince Henry event, and clashing with the Czar Nicholas Touring Trials in Russia, works participation was poor. Even amongst the major Austrian manufacturers there was only Laurin & Klement, as both Austro-Daimler and RAF had concentrated all their efforts on the important Prince Henry Trial in Germany. The 1st Alpine Trial was a 535 mile event starting and finishing in Vienna. Amongst the numerous mountain passes the dreaded Katschberg was the most difficult to conquer. Only six cars arrived without penalty points and, not unexpectedly, Laurin & Klement won the Team prize with the three cars of Counts Paul Draskovich and Alexander Kolowrat, as well as the 1903 La Turbie winner Otto Hieronimus. The lowest petrol consumption was rewarded with a special prize of 1500 Crowns and went to Louis Obruba and his Mathis.

For Margrave Alexander Pallavicini, President of the Austrian Automobile Club, June 1910 was full of surprises, good and bad. These began on 7th June with the triple win of the

Austrian Daimler cars in the Prince Henry Trials. Then came the Royal Warrant: on 17th June the 80 year old Emperor Franz Joseph graciously upgraded the Club to make it the 'Imperial Royal Austrian Automobile Club'. Yet this favour did not prevent the bad news of June 21st when the Governor of Lower Austria, for safety reasons, refused permission to organize the traditional Semmering Hill Climb, held annually since 1899. For the Club it was a terrible shock, coming only five days before the start of the Alpine Trial. This mishap, however, provoked the decision to develop the 1911 Alpine into a true successor to the Prince Henry Trials.

The 2nd Alpine Trial, held in May 1911, was over a distance of 1421 kilometres (883 miles) and included the Katschberg and Loibl Passes, the latter with a gradient of almost one in three. When competitors assembled in Vienna observers noticed that artillery wheels had almost disappeared, being replaced by the more modern wire wheels. 51 cars were sent on their way, and 41 of them arrived at the finish in Vienna, only 12 with a clean sheet. The emphasis was again on team performance, and the three works Austro-Daimlers came home without dropping a single point. The team was the same as that which won the 1910 Prince Henry Trial: Ferdinand Porsche, Eduard Fischer, and Count Heinrich Schönfeldt. The press hailed it as 'the Iron Team', and Austro-Daimler was quick to bring out a series of replicas under the name of 'Alpenwagen'. Second place in the team competition went to the three works Laurin & Klements, driven by Otto Hieronimus (with a clean sheet) as well as Counts Draskovich and Kolowrat (with a few penalty points each). The Audi Team – August Horch's new make – was third (Horch unpenalised, team-mates Hans Zeidler and Alexander Graumüller having dropped points).

Two more Austro-Daimlers, one Puch, and an NAG also finished without loss of marks, just like the two Nesselsdorf (later Tatra) cars driven by Fritz Hückel and design chief

Laurin & Klement design chief Otto Hieronimus, outright winner of the 1903 La Turbie Hill Climb in France, at the wheel of his car, having a rest at the top of Katschberg in the 1910 Alpine. Sitting on the running board (inside the spare wheel, goggles on his cap) is an interested observer from Austro-Daimler named Ferdinand Porsche, just back from that make's triple win in the 1910 Prince Henry Trial.

Ferdinand Porsche at Loiblpass on a recce for the 1911 Alpine in his Austro-Daimler, accompanied by his wife Aloysia, née Kaes. That year the Team Prize went to Austro-Daimler.

Hans Ledwinka. The entrant of Ledwinka's Nesselsdorf was Valentin Kadlczik who also entered a 25hp Coventry Daimler with sleeve valve Knight engine. For the Alpine Kadlczik procured an experienced trials driver (a Mr Bush) from the British Daimler works. After the event, when interviewed by *Allgemeine Automobil Zeitung,* Mr Bush said: "Some years ago I participated in the Herkomer Trial (1906) but the (Herkomer) route was nowhere near as difficult as the Alpine passes. People here tried to make me afraid but I was very sure of my car. ... At the Loibl (pass) the radiator stayed so cool that I could touch it with my cheek."

Alec de Villeroy from France experienced the Alpine at the wheel of a works-supported Austro-Daimler. His comment highlights the Automobile Club de France's one-sided preference for races, as distinct from trials:

"Your Alpine Trial followed an original concept. To my knowledge nowhere the question of staging competitions for genuine touring cars was so well solved as by the Sporting Commission of the Austrian Automobile Club. In France events of this kind are unknown."

For 1912 the distance was increased to seven stages with a total of 1468 miles. And the Austrian Club followed the example of the Herkomer and Prince Henry Trials, with the Great Alpine Challenge Trophy, another huge piece of silverware. It was to be awarded to the entrant with the smallest number of accumulated penalty points in the Alpine Trials of 1912, 1913 and 1914. No less than 17 three-car factory teams were entered for the event, and there were 85 starters from eight countries. But very soon one team after the other collected penalty marks on one or more of their three cars. Austro-Daimler, Laurin & Klement, Audi, and the two official Benz Teams were amongst the serious contenders who failed. Finally, there were only two teams left with clean sheets, the German Opel Team of Fritz Opel, Carl Joerns and Robert Koch, and the team of the Austrian Fiat Works in Vienna, driven by Giovanni Marcellino, Baron Hans von Veyder-Malberg, and Karl Bettaque (the latter did have a few penalty points of the second category which did not count for the Team Award). They both received a Team Prize of equal value and importance. A happy Fritz Opel, 3rd of the Opel brothers, then announced: "This greatest sporting event of the year was the most difficult of all the reliability trials ever held."

Carl Joerns, the Opel Grand Prix driver, member of the 1912 winning Opel Team (Fritz Opel was driving a similar car).

The Archduke Karl Franz Josef in his Austro-Daimler finished the 1912 Alpine without loss of marks, with chauffeur Gregoric at the wheel. In 1916 Karl Franz Josef succeeded to the Austro-Hungarian throne as Emperor Karl I, but died in exile in 1922.

The Austrian Fiat Company expressed its satisfaction with the Team Award by speedily marketing a new model, the 24/28hp Fiat Alpenwagen. Altogether no less than 25 cars arrived at the finish with a clean sheet. The most prominent of the them were two private Austro-Daimler entrants, the brothers-in-law Archduke Karl Franz Joseph and Prince Elias of Bourbon-Parma. In 1916 the Archduke was to become Emperor Charles I of Austria, and his wife, later Empress Zita, was Prince Elias's sister. You can call it one-upmanship over the participation of Prince Henry of Prussia in the Herkomer Trials ...

Other competitors were less fortunate. Miss Helene Morariu-Andriewitsch was a student of philosophy and the first female to tackle the Alpine. On the 5th stage her Puch hit a stone block and she had to retire. Charles L Freeston,

correspondent of *The Autocar* and author of the book *The High Roads of the Alps*, also pranged his car. He was not competing, but following the Trial was no less hazardous. He collided with an Italian Züst car driven by another non-competitor. Worse still, Freeston became the bearer of bad news: his was the sad duty to report the regrettable fact that the only British car entered, James Radley's Rolls-Royce Silver Ghost, had failed to negotiate the very steep gradient at Katschberg. Rolls-Royce was terribly proud of its 40/50 model which, in 1911, had gone from London to Edinburgh without ever changing down from top (third) gear, with a resultant fuel economy of 24.3mpg, yet was able to reach a speed of 126km/h (78.2mph) at Brooklands. Laudable as this may have been, it was not the right gearing for the Austrian Alps.

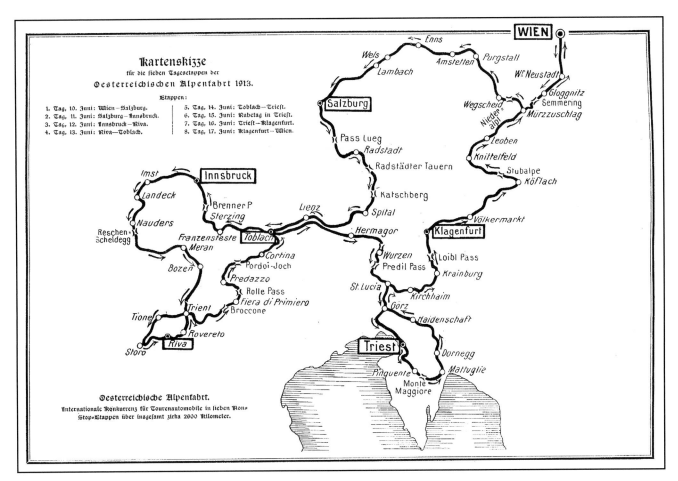

The 1660 mile itinerary of the 1913 Great Austrian Alpine Tour.

Works participation in the Alpine was a costly undertaking, and the Austrian motor manufacturers and traders signed something like a boycott agreement to abstain from works participation in 1913. This provoked a little crisis as there were only 43 starters. However, the Trial was extended to eight non-stop stages making a total of 1657 miles. The number of works teams competing for the Team Prize was down to six: three German makes (Audi, Hansa, and Horch), the Swiss sleeve valve Fischers, the Belgian Minervas, and Rolls-Royce, thirsting for revenge. Four Rolls-Royce 'Continentals' were entered, each with four speed gearbox and higher performance, for private entrant James Radley, as well as the works drivers Ernest Walter Hives, JK 'Jock' Sinclair, and Curt Cornelius Friese, the Rolls-Royce agent in Vienna. Eric Platford, returning from the Spanish Grand Prix where he won third place, was there as team manager, and Claude Johnson's presence signified the importance of the occasion.

The Fischer and Minerva Teams each suffered from some retirements, so that only four complete teams returned to Vienna, out of a total of 31 cars still running. The Horch and Hansa Teams were loaded with hundreds of penalty points, so the decision was a very close one between Rolls-Royce and Audi. Again, there were three grades of penalty points (according to the gravity of the default), which made things a bit complicated. Friese (Rolls-Royce) and the two works Audis of Lange and Graumüller could present completely clean sheets, whilst August Horch's Audi lost 8 points of the second category against Hives's 3, and Radley's 9 of the third category. The duel was decided by the two points of the first category which Jock Sinclair's Rolls-Royce had collected on the second leg. Thus, the Team prize went to Audi by a tiny margin. Both companies rejoiced. Audi introduced a replica model for sale, the Audi 'Alpensieger', and the Rolls-Royce Continental became the 'Alpine Eagle'. For Ernest Walter Hives the Alpine was an important stepping stone in his career with Rolls-Royce. In 1931 he became Managing Director and, in 1950, Lord Hives of Hazeldene.

The previous year's lady driver had acquired a husband and now called herself Mrs Helene von Stamati-Morariu. She had a penalty-free run in her Puch and hoped for a first class award. However, in the final scrutineering a broken spring was discovered, and a penalty inflicted. Undeterred, the Puch Company quickly launched an 'Alpenwagen' of which no less than 1850 were sold in the years to come. Only nine cars had come through with flying colours: the works Audis of Lange and Graumüller, as well as the private entry of Louis Obruba; Friese (Rolls-Royce), Georg Paulmann (Horch), Sylvain de Jong (Minerva), Walter Delmár (Benz), Johann Sirutschek (Raaba), and the privately entered Laurin & Klement of Count Kolowrat, driven by Otto Hieronimus.

Before the start of the 1914 Alpine Trial the big question was who would finally win the Challenge Trophy, called 'der

Opposite: Rolls-Royce, thirsting for revenge, lined up four cars – and all of them finished the Alpine Trial.

Grosse Alpen-Wanderpreis'? The distance of the trial was increased to 1821 miles, a total of eight daily stages. The 75 starters had to conquer a total of 30 Alpine passes, including Turracher Höhe, steeper still than the dreaded Katschberg. To rule out ultra-low transmissions there was also a 10 kilometre speed test at Wels in Upper Austria. Charles Freeston, by now an expert on the Austrian Alpine, wrote in the 27th June edition of *The Autocar*: "Frankly, I am bound to say that in all my motoring experiences, extending over fifteen years, I have never known anything so arduous as the first day's run of the Austrian Alpine Contest of 1914: It was terrific."

At the Innsbruck overnight stop James Radley in his Rolls-Royce Alpine Eagle arrived first, leading the entire field. There the great sportsman was told horror stories of Turracher Höhe with its gradient of 1 in 3, to be tackled the next day. As there were no Rolls-Royce works entries, Radley was on his own. Luckily, Charles Freeston had been issued with a Rolls-Royce press car which Radley quickly borrowed. He set out on a successful recce to Turracher Höhe, drove all night over 400 miles of mountain roads, and just managed to get back to Innsbruck in time for the start in the morning.

When the battle was finally over and 50 cars had safely arrived at the finish in Vienna, two works teams qualified for a Team Award of equal standing: August Horch, Alexander Graumüller, and Hermann Lange constituted the Audi Team, while the Hansa works cars were driven by Albin Kappel, Ing Garais and Karl Köhler. Replicas of the successful F-type Hansa were quickly named 'Alpentyp'!

A total of 19 cars retained clean sheets, which was remarkable. One of them was James Radley's car – he had finally made it at the third attempt! There were quite a number of British works and individual entries. Freeston's reports and Rolls-Royce publicity had established the Alpine Trial as a very important event in English minds. Herbert Austin entered a 3160cc Austin, with Kendall as chauffeur and Herbert Austin Jr as mechanic. It had a trouble-free run for seven days, but in the eighth daily stage lost 14 points. Despite this they were awarded a Silver medal. Exactly 50 years later, in 1964, Paddy Hopkirk would be the outright winner of the Austrian Alpine

The Rolls-Royce Team (l to r): Ernest Walter Hives, team manager Eric Platford, EC Parsons (mechanic), Jock Sinclair, James Radley and Curt Cornelius Friese (who brought R 1706 home with a clean sheet). Rolls-Royce managing director Claude Goodman Johnson was also there but not in the picture.

Rally in an Austin-Healey 3000. Tinsley Waterhouse in his Vauxhall (3970cc) dropped 25 points in the third stage and also qualified for a Silver Medal, as did HM Ainsworth (4 litre Hotchkiss), with 134 points.

The team of three American Cadillacs with 6 litre engines, British-entered by FS Bennett Ltd of London, did not quite feel at home in the Alps, and only Alfred Maynard won a Silver Medal although loaded with penalties. The other two cars were eliminated yet "drove to the finish under official control", receiving Bronze Medals as a consolation. Mrs Boston, the sister of the famous conductor Sir Thomas Beecham, ran out of road but was stopped from overturning by the stone marker she hit. When her Cadillac was roadworthy again the gallant lady, accompanied by entrant Frederic Bennett, insisted on driving to the finish in Vienna, so her medal certainly was well merited.

The smallest car in the field, a works-entered Singer 1100 driven by EL Roberts, also continued after elimination with the result of a Bronze Medal. Sir Edward Duncombe in his 3 litre Wolseley gave up soon after the start, while G Slaney in a works-entered Armstrong-Whitworth 3.8 litre had a trouble-free run, without losing one single point for seven days, but then had the hard luck to be forced out on the very last leg.

When the Austrian Automobile Club had offered its Challenge Trophy it had seemed impossible for anyone to have a penalty-free run in three consecutive years! But the reliability standards had risen fantastically, and now the club was confronted with five competitors who had an equal right to the Challenge Trophy with its material value of 10,000 Austrian Kronen, or the price of a luxury car. They were Graumüller and Lange (both Audis), Louis Obruba (Mathis in 1912, Audi in 1913/14), Sylvain de Jong, founder and director of the Belgian Minerva Company, and Count Alexander Kolowrat (Laurin &

The first Alpine Trials 1910-1914

With Alexander Graumüller its outstanding driver, Audi snatched the 1913 Team Prize from Rolls-Royce by a small margin.

Klement). August Horch shouted loudest, but the others would not give in. The excitement mounted, the Club proposed to draw lots, but finally it was agreed that the Club should keep the original, with copies going to the five winners, an expensive proposition. Thus peace and calm was re-established.

"On 27th June we started our return trip to Zwickau", wrote August Horch in his memoirs. Next day in Sarajevo Gavrilo Princip fired the starting shot for the Kaiser War, assassinating the Austrian heir-apparent, the Archduke Franz Ferdinand. It was the end of an era.

By the time the 1918 ceasefire came, ten million people had perished in the war, the three Emperors of Russia, Germany, and Austria had lost their thrones, and the complete break-up of the Austro-Hungarian Empire by the Treaties of St Germain and Trianon, judged a "cardinal tragedy" by Winston S Churchill, left but the tiny republic of Austria with a population of 6 million out of originally 54 million. With this, the Alpenfahrt went down the drain, as important parts of its itinerary (like the Dolomites) had passed to other countries. However, the loss of the Alpine Trial was neither the prime concern of the starving little country nor Churchill's who maintained that "there is not one of the peoples or provinces that constituted the Empire of the Habsburgs to whom gaining

Who was to win the Great Alpine Challenge Trophy – that was the question in 1914.

their independence has not brought the tortures which ancient poets and theologians had reserved for the damned".

It took no less than five years for a half-hearted effort to recreate the Alpine. An Austro-Hungarian Trial was held in 1923 which first took in the Austrian Alps before going into the Hungarian plains. Hungarian Walter Delmár in an Austrian

In 1914 James Radley was back with a solitary Rolls-Royce. He finished with a clean sheet and put up the fastest time of the day in each of the special tests.

Steyr car was the outright winner. Right after the finish some aristocratic participants then spontaneously organized a Vienna to Salzburg Gesellschafts-Alpenfahrt, or Alpine Society Trial. It did attract one Mercedes works entry, though, but its pilot retired at Katschberg with rear axle trouble. His name, incidentally, was Alfred Neubauer. Count Rudolf Kinsky was the outright winner in his 3.3 litre Steyr, but fastest time of day at Katschberg went to Baron Friedrich von Mayr-Melnhof in his Rolls-Royce.

The success of these two events led to the creation of the 1924 Alföld-Alpenfahrt. Combining flat Puszta and mountainous Alpine roads, it was run in seven stages over a distance of 1379 miles, with two speed tests, as well as hill climbs at Katschberg and Präbichl. The field took off in Budapest, and 37 cars reached the finish in Vienna, 21 of them with bonus points. Baron Hans von Veyder-Malberg (Austro-Daimler) tied with Rudolf Kinsky's eldest brother Count Ulrich Kinsky (Steyr) for the outright win. The latter soon became a formidable racing driver specializing in hill climbs. His great-uncle Count Charles Kinsky, lover of Lady Randolph Churchill, had won the 1883 Liverpool Steeple Chase.

The Manufacturers Team Prize for Touring Cars went to the Steyr Team, composed of Count Heinrich Schönfeldt, Walter Delmár and Ladislaus von Almásy. Incidentally, the story of the latter's adventurous life in North Africa was the stuff from which Michael Ondaatje formed his well-known novel *The English Patient*. The Voiturette Team Award was won by Nesselsdorf/Tatra (Josef Vermirovský, Franz Bittmann, and Josef Cservenka).

In all those postwar years the Austrians closely watched developments in Italy where the 'Coppa delle Alpi' was run over formerly Austrian Alpine passes. And all of a sudden the idea was born to merge the various national Alpine Trials into something bigger, something resembling the Great Austrian Alpine Tour of pre-war days. To prepare for such a development, ÖAC in 1925 organized an Austrian Alpine Trial, and the cooperation of the Bavarians was sought. The event started in Vienna, finished in Munich, and in between it was the real thing. As August Horch, who attended as an observer, recalled in his memoirs, in pouring rain not a single car managed to climb Turracher Höhe without the aid of snow chains. There were speed hill climbs at Katschberg and Tauernpass, plus speed tests on the straights of Neunkirchner Allee and Forstenrieder Park. Count Ulrich Kinsky (Steyr) was fastest at Katschberg, but he did not finish this Alpine. The Steyr Company asked him to retire and to proceed to Montlhéry for the 1925 French Touring Car Grand Prix immediately. There he put up the fastest lap. But the Alpine continued and the Gräf & Stift of Karl Gruber was fastest at Tauernpass. Both speed tests went to Baron Philipp Berckheim in his supercharged Mercedes. Of the 41 starters, only 17 cars reached Munich, and 4 of them were rewarded with Alpine Cups for penalty-free runs. The special tests acted as tie deciders amongst them. Thus, top honours went to the veteran Count Heinrich Schönfeldt, hero of the 1910 Prince Henry Trial and the 1911 Alpenfahrt, in a Steyr VII. Second was Rudolf Reinicke, of Germany, in his Presto, ahead of Walter Delmár (Hungary) and Baron Leo Haan (both Steyr VII).

It was a good Trial but it could not, of course, measure up to the great pre-war events so strongly supported by the motor industry of numerous countries. To catch the aura of the old Alpine and revive it was beyond little Austria's capabilities. It could not be done alone, but now there was a flicker of hope ...

The first Alpine Trials 1910-1914

In 1914 Mrs Boston, sister of Britain's famous conductor Sir Thomas Beecham, was the first British lady driver to participate in the Alpine. Although hitting a stone marker with her Cadillac she continued to the finish "under official control" and was awarded a bronze medal. She was not the first lady to enter the Rally, however, because, in 1912 and 1913, Fräulein Helene Morariu had taken part in the Alpine in her Puch car, and finished the event in 1913.

Five drivers finished the 1912, 1913 and 1914 Alpine without loss of marks, and, therefore, had equal rights to the Great Alpine Challenge Trophy. Finally, copies had to be made for each one of them. They were Hermann Lange (Audi), Alexander Graumüller (Audi), Sylvain de Jong (Minerva), Louis Obruba (Mathis and Audi), and Count Alexander Kolowrat (Laurin & Klement).

A Pan-European effort
1928-1936

Italy, one of the victors of World War I, had annexed some of Austria's most beautiful Alpine provinces, such as South Tyrol and the entire Trieste region. Taking pride in these new possessions, and making use of an already illustrious name, the Automobile Club di Milano, quickly created the 'Coppa delle Alpi'. It was first held in 1921, started in Milan and took competitors to night stops in Torino, Merano, Trieste, Trento, and back to Milan, over a distance of 1430 miles. The Trial not only tackled the mountains in Piemonte and the region north of Milan bordering on Switzerland, but it also included the prize sections of the old Austrian Alpine, including the Stelvio, the Dolomites and the mountain passes north of Trieste.

It was a very ambitious project, and the Austrian *Allgemeine Automobil Zeitung* commented on "the Italian Alpine Trial which, in a sense, was the heir of the Austrian Alpenfahrt".

Entries were mainly Italian, but Mercedes sent four cars, and the irrepressible Count Alexander Kolowrat entered an Austro-Daimler. There was also one Laurin & Klement entry, no longer Austrian but coming from the newly created republic of Czechoslovakia. Finally, 25 cars took to the road, to cover the distance at a prescribed average speed of 30mph. Penalties were inflicted both for lateness and for exceeding 31mph. After the first leg (at Torino) ten cars were still unpenalized, three

At the age of 25 Enzo Ferrari was fourth overall and class winner in the 1923 Coppa delle Alpi driving a 20-30 ES Alfa Romeo.

Itala, two Ceirano (all in the 3 litre class), one Alfa Romeo, one SPA (both 4½ litres), two Mercedes and one Lancia (both unlimited). Soon after the start of the second stage Alfred Vischer, son of the late Gustav Vischer (Daimler Board Member) retired his Mercedes with a broken front wheel, and there were more losses to come. Only 14 cars reached the overnight stop at Merano. Those were the men, as distinct from the boys, and they mastered both the gruelling Dolomite stage and

Antonio Ascari (Alfa Romeo), a serious contender to win the first Coppa delle Alpi of 1921, rammed a bridge on the last stage and retired.

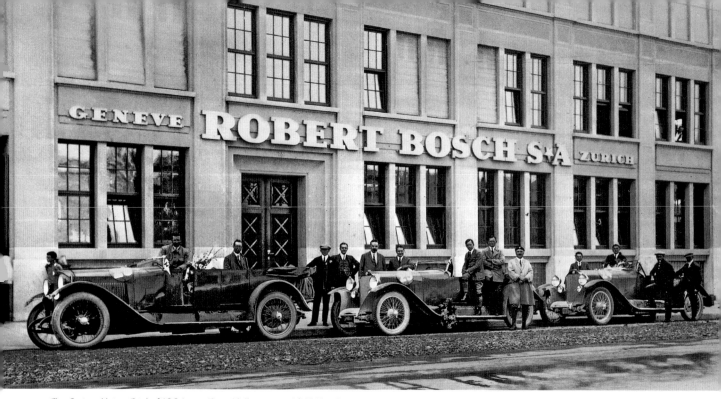

The Swiss Alpine Trial of 1924 saw Fritz Nallinger in a 16/50hp Benz victorious, with team-mate Schürch second overall. The photo shows the three Benz cars of Nallinger, Schürch and E Muhl (12th place) in front of the Bosch building in Geneva.

the Alpi Orientali near Trieste with remarkably few incidents. On the last leg from Trento to Milan Antonio Ascari had a nasty crash when his Alfa Romeo left the road going over a bridge. Max Sailer (Mercedes) helped the crew in their predicament. With Ascari out of the race, there were nine cars at the finish, three of them without loss of marks, two Italas in the 3 litre class (Claudio Sandonnino and Giuseppe Rebuffo) and Ferdinando Minoia (Mercedes, over 4500cc unlimited). In case of a tie the rules gave precedence to the car with the smaller engine. The Alpine Cup and the first two places, therefore, went to Itala, Mercedes being third. Ugo Sivocci and Enzo Ferrari (both Alfa Romeo ES Sport 4¼ litre) were fourth and fifth overall, after Sailer (Mercedes) was eliminated from fifth position following protests.

For 1922 the distance was increased to 1720 miles, and 13 out of 37 starters arrived at the finish in Milan – all Italians. The outright winner was Pietro Cattaneo driving an Italian Ceirano car, with Rebuffo (Itala) the runner-up. Next year there were 44 starters, 25 of them making it into the results list after a journey of 1826 miles. Only four cars never deviated from the stipulated average speed, so again top honours went to the smallest of them: first place and the Alpine Cup went to Ferdinando Minoia driving a type 469 OM of 1469cc. Pietro Garro and Eugenio Beria d'Argentina, both in type S23 SPA cars of 2724cc, were ranked second and third ahead of Enzo Ferrari (Alfa Romeo RL SS, 2994cc). The other class winners, apart from the glorious Minoia/1500 and Garro/3000, were Meo Constantini (Amilcar, 1100) and Carlo Bucchetti (Ansaldo, 2000). For the first time there was also a class for military officers, won by Capitano Torti in a Fiat. Still, the Coppa delle Alpi had not yet achieved a breakthrough. It had become a major national event, though, all the participants being Italian, and Meo Constantini's Amilcar 1100 was the only non-Italian car in the field!

Was it wishful thinking when *Allgemeine Automobil Zeitung* proclaimed the inevitable advent of a truly supranational Alpine Trial in the more distant future? It stated, however, that there was no hope for 1924, as preparations for both the Coppa delle Alpi and a Swiss Alpine Trial were already too far advanced. Yes, the Automobile Club of Switzerland had made up its mind to stage a Swiss Alpine, a forerunner of which had been held once before, in 1914. The Swiss Competitions Committee tried successfully to attract competitors from many nations. In fact, there were cars and drivers from Austria, Belgium, France, Germany, Switzerland and Hungary. What a difference when compared with the Coppa delle Alpi! The Swiss Alpine also included two special tests, a 'novelty' the Italians declined to introduce into their event. There were 17 finishers in the 1924 Swiss Alpine, and Benz cars took a double victory. The outright winner was Fritz Nallinger, later to become a prominent Board Member of Daimler-Benz. Close behind Schürch in the second Benz was Poulin in his Citroën. Then came three Belgian Minerva cars driven by Edgar Goujon, Sylvain de Jong, and Marmini, which meant that Minerva also pocketed the Team Award. Fastest in the Hill Climb, and seventh overall, was Baron Hans von Veyder-Malberg in a Steyr. The speed test over the kilometre went to B Schriever driving a French Bignan car.

Austria and Hungary combined forces to run the 1924 Alföld-Alpenfahrt described earlier, and then there was the 4th Coppa delle Alpi. Participation was down to 20 starters, and there were nine finishers. The increased distance – 1758 miles – did nothing to uprate the event. OM took the first two places (Vincenzo Coffani ahead of Nando Minoia), with Cesare Schieppati third in an Italian Diatto. The side show for the military over a reduced distance of 745 miles was won by Capitano Papa driving another OM.

1925 saw the Austrian Alpine finish in Munich, so as to generate interest for the event in Germany. The Coppa delle Alpi, however, experienced a further erosion of its international standing. There were 24 starters, with Filippo Tassara (Bugatti 1500) the overall winner, and Felice Bianchi Anderloni (Peugeot) scoring an 1100cc class win. The class for military officers was won by Capitano Guerrini driving an OM, while 'other ranks' were issued with Fiat lorries to take some motoring exercise ...

Over five years the AC di Milano had successfully developed the Coppa delle Alpi but failed to attract the European motor industry. Now the Club came to realize that supranational cooperation was needed to create a truly International Alpine Trial. It would have to transcend all national borders, the way the Alps do. Preliminary talks were held with the Austrian Automobile Club, the only other club with long standing Alpine Trials experience. Then, on the occasion of the AIACR General Assembly in Paris on May 5th 1925, a meeting took place of the Austrian, French, German, Italian and Swiss National Clubs. Italy did the next step and invited the other four countries to Milan where, on September 5th, it presented a concept for a joint Alpine event to be held in 1926. An organizing committee was set up. In October draft regulations were submitted by the Italians, though perhaps in a bit of a 'take-it-or-leave-it' manner. This was not very well received and strongly divergent opinions were voiced. Austria opted out first, to pursue its own ideas in another combination. The ACF was lukewarm as racing prevailed in France and trials were almost unknown there. When the remaining four countries failed to reach an agreement, Italy launched the idea of a Gran Premio d'Italia della Montagna. However, just like the Austro-Yugoslav Alpine Trial with Vienna, Belgrade and Ragusa/Dubrovnik as the corner stones, it was cancelled.

Thus it was that, in 1926, nothing was achieved but a big Alpine void, and it was only in 1927 that the gaps between the clubs involved was bridged. The difficulties were enormous, and the beautiful dream, the 1st International Alpine Trial (Coupe Internationale des Alpes) only saw the light of day in August 1928.

With France abstaining, the organizing countries were Italy, Germany, Austria, and Switzerland. There was general agreement that the event should start in Milan, but Munich won over Vienna as the final destination. As distinct from the penalty points system of the pre-war Austrian Alpine Tour, minimum and maximum speeds according to cubic capacity classes were laid down. Not achieving the minimum speed meant exclusion, and there were bonuses for exceeding the minimum speed, up to the maximum. 84 cars, mainly from Italy and Germany, departed from Milan. In conformity with the Italian concept there were no special tests, but the Trial certainly was not the type of "comfort race across Europe" the way the Monte Carlo Rally saw itself in those early years.

After 1095 miles of mountain roads in Italy, Switzerland, Austria, and Southern Germany, 59 cars arrived in Munich. 44 of them were classified. The fastest and 'raciest' cars of the entire field certainly were the Italian two litre OM two-seaters, driven by 1927 Mille Miglia-winner Giuseppe Morandi, Vincenzo Coffani, and Antonio Masperi. OM won one of the

The 1929 International Alpine brought the first major BMW success on four wheels. The winning team of Max Buchner, Albert Kandt Jr and Willy Wagner won an Alpine Cup. The tiny BMW Dixi cars were based on the Austin Seven and built at Eisenach under licence.

Austrian Fritz von Zsolnay, winner of the Semmering Hill Climb in 1927, returned from the first International Alpine (1928) with a clean sheet and an Alpine Cup, driving a Gräf & Stift.

four Alpine Cups awarded to One-Make Teams. The other two litre team was the Belgian Minervas (Leopold Roger, René van Parys, and Edgar Goujon), a fitting tribute to Minerva founder Sylvain de Jong who passed away that year. De Jong, it will be recalled, was one of the five ex-aequo winners of the Great Alpine Challenge Trophy of 1914. Two teams in the three litre class took the remaining Alpine Cups, both going to German makes, Adler (Otto Löhr, André Dewald, and Hans Coenen) and Brennabor. The team of this little-known manufacturer of Brandenburg, near Berlin, was captained by Fritz Backasch, who had driven a works Brennabor into 11th place at the 1926 German Grand Prix, held at AVUS and won by Caracciola in a Mercedes. The other cars were driven by Hans Niedlich and Fritz Lehnert. Those 1928 'Coupes Internationales des Alpes' weren't really cups at all, they were replicas of the 2000 years old nymph 'Danaide' found in a museum in Rome. And they came in two sizes, big ones for the teams, and smaller ones for individual entrants.

Nineteen of these also obtained maximum bonus points and were consequently awarded small-sized Alpine Cups, or rather, Nymphlets. Six of them went to cars above three litres, the only ones

Soon to become an international celebrity Rudolf Caracciola won an Alpine goblet in the 1929 International Alpine, driving a type Nürburg Mercedes. He is followed here by Willy Walb in a similar car.

that had to have four seats, such as the 7.8 litre Gräf & Stift driven by Austrian hillclimb specialist Fritz von Zsolnay. Only two Alpine Cups went to drivers of British makes, Austrians Hans Georg Koch in his 2230cc Standard Six and Dr Oskar Schmidt (Talbot 1500). British participation, in fact, was limited to the Hon Mildred Mary Bruce who, in December 1927, together with her husband, had set 17 long distance records at Montlhéry. Entering the same two litre AC for the Alpine Trial, she had the bad luck to be 'torpedoed' by an official car in the second daily stage. As a token of the organizers' repentance she was permitted to have the AC repaired, to continue to the finish, and to receive a Gold Medal "honoris causa"!

As Major Leo Czermak, Vice President of Automobil Club von Deutschland, emphasized in his speech at the prize-giving, the International Alpine Trial was the very first motor sports event ever organized jointly by four National Clubs. Considering the resulting language and organizational difficulties one must attest that it was a good beginning, yet there was still room for further improvement.

1929 brought the second Coupe Internationale des Alpes. It was again organized by Automobil Club von Deutschland and Reale Automobile Club d'Italia, with the Austrian and Swiss Clubs as junior partners. 80 cars – out of 95 entries – started in Munich, to cover a distance of 1557 miles through those four countries. There were two timed hill climbs in Italy, Stelvio and Pordoi, where maximum times were fixed for each one of the three classes (1100, 3000, and unlimited). Penalty marks were inflicted on anyone slower than these standards, as well as for delays en route. Fastest time of day at the Stelvio was put up by Georg Kimpel (16min 29sec), ahead of Wilhelm Merck (17min 14sec, both Mercedes SSKs). Third and fourth fastest were Emilio Ricchetti (Bugatti, 17min 38sec) from Trieste and the Polish Count Adam Potocki (Austro-Daimler, 17min 51sec), both running in the 3 litre class. At the Pordoi, the order was Kimpel (10min 19sec) ahead of Ricchetti (10min 54sec) and Carlo Salamano (Fiat, 10min 56sec). The beautiful setting of the Villa d'Este on Lake Como had been selected as the finish, and 48 cars arrived there.

One Alpine Cup each was awarded to the winning manufacturers' teams in the 1100cc and in the unlimited class. For BMW in the 1100cc class this was the first major trophy for a success on four wheels. The three BMW Dixi cars driven by

Max Buchner, Albert Kandt, and Willy Wagner finished the Trial at the prescribed average speed of 26mph (42kph). This was quite an achievement which observers did not at all expect. The Dixi cars were actually Austin Sevens built under licence at the Eisenach works.

The winning Hansa Team, however, had to – and did – meet the average speed of 30mph (48kph) stipulated for the unlimited class. It was the Hansa swan song, a proud make created by August Sporkhorst in 1905. Now his two sons Fredo and Ernst Werner, as well as Eduard Hörbe in the third car, finished the Trial with a fine performance to win the last major trophy for Hansa. The make disappeared when taken over by Borgward.

The 36 unpenalized individual entrants and drivers received 'Alpenbecher' or Alpine Goblets. Mercedes drivers won eight, those of Ford and Wanderer five each. Altogether, 19 of those Alpenbechers went to German makes, 8 to American, 7 to Italian, and one each to French (Bugatti, driver Ricchetti) and Austrian (Austro-Daimler, driver Desiderius von Bitzy) brands. There were no French entries, and the two from Britain (Victor E Leverett, Arrol-Aster 3257cc and Roy Franey, Riley 1089cc) both retired.

Clearly, the French and the British had not yet discovered the charm of the International Alpine Trial but perhaps it needed a pause to achieve just that. Following Wall Street's Black Friday there was no International Alpine Trial in 1930. Surprisingly, two small countries stepped in to fill the gap with their own Alpine Trials. Euphoric over Hans Stuck who was well on his way to win the first ever European Hill Climb Championship for Austro-Daimler, the Austrians organized their own 'Austrian Alpine Cup' and, four weeks later, a joint venture with the Hungarians, a new edition of 'Alföld-Alpenfahrt'.

36 cars tackled the 'Austrian Alpine Cup', with hill climbs at Josefsberg, Triebener Tauern, and Arlberg, all of them won by Desiderius von Bitzy's Austro-Daimler ADR 3 litre. He was the undisputed head of a newly formed Austro-Daimler Team of three Austrian gentleman drivers. The others were Count Felix Spiegel and the steel magnate Philipp von Schoeller. Of the 9 Alpine Cups attributed for clean sheets, five went to Austro-Daimler (including the aforementioned team, of course). The only British entrant was Donald Healey driving

an Invicta, and both driver and car took to the Alps like fish to water. This earned Healey an Alpine Cup. Legend has it that for the 1930 Alpine outings Donald Healey borrowed a fast 3 litre Invicta from Miss Violet Cordery (of Monza and Montlhéry record fame) yet the Alföld-Alpenfahrt entry list says 'Invicta 4429ccm'. The young Invicta make needed publicity, so Noel Macklin, the man behind Invicta, opted for trials and rallies to make the brand known internationally. The two 1930 trials in Austria and Hungary were the beginning, and others would follow. Therefore, it seems quite plausible that the smaller 3 litre record car of Macklin's sister-in-law was also requisitioned for this purpose.

Then came the Alföld-Alpenfahrt. 36 touring and 4 sports cars departed Vienna to tackle the Alps, including a speed hill climb at Pötschen Pass, before moving on to the Hungarian plains. The Trial finished in Budapest where an acceleration and braking test was held in front of the Technical College, the 'Polytechnikum'. There, Hans Lieser in a Talbot put up fastest time of the day, ahead of Ladislaus Balazs in a Hungarian Magosix. The test also acted as tie decider for general classification amongst the 15 cars that had completed the Trial with a clean sheet. As Lieser had received penalty marks he was not eligible, and Ladislaus Balazs became the outright winner, with Count Manó Andrássy (Tatra) second and Desiderius von Bitzy (Austro-Daimler) third. Two British drivers were amongst the 15 winners of Alföld-Alpine Cups, Donald Healey (Invicta) in 6th and Shelagh Brunner (Austro-Daimler) – married to Prince Ferdinand Liechtenstein – in 11th place overall. She also won the Ladies Prize. There was a tie for the coveted Manufacturers Team Prize between Austro-Daimler (Desiderius von Bitzy, Philipp von Schoeller, and Count Felix Spiegel) and Gräf & Stift (Franz Pauker, Josef Gräf, and Gustav Schimatzek).

With two Alpine Cups in the bag Donald Healey had become quite a celebrity. When interviewed by *AAZ* in Budapest he said he liked the first event better because the more glamorous Alföld-Alpenfahrt contained too many miles of uninspiring main roads in the Hungarian plains. The English media also took up his success story (reinforced by his outright win in the 1931 Monte), and all of a sudden the Alpine Trials were established as important events in British minds. When the International Alpine Trial was resumed in 1931 as the 3ème

Winning a Team Prize in the 1930 Alföld-Alpenfahrt, the Austro-Daimler team is lined up in front of St Stephen's Monument in Budapest, (l to r) Count Felix Spiegel-Diesenberg, steel magnate Philipp von Schoeller (both ADR 3 litre models) and Desiderius von Bitzy driving the latest 3.6 litre Bergmeister model.

Coupe Internationale des Alpes, the British were there in force. It was clearly defined now that Manufacturers Teams would compete for Alpine Cups, while there were Glacier Cups for individual entrants. The most valuable development was the inclusion of an important stage in the French Alps, and the ACF sent a delegate to observe the event. Thus, for the first time, the itinerary encompassed all the famous Alpine passes regardless of national frontiers. There were 72 entries, and 62 cars were actually sent on their way in Munich, to compete in the three classes up to 1100, to 3000, and over 3000cc. The 1468 miles itinerary included timed hill climbs at the Stelvio and the Col du Galibier. It covered Germany, Austria, Italy, France, and Switzerland where the Trial ended in the Federal Capital of Berne, as the 1931 event was held under the chairmanship of the Swiss Automobile Club. It is remarkable that 44 cars reached the finish line.

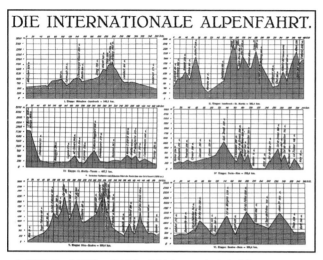

In 1931 the 2405km (1494 mile) itinerary included five countries (Germany, Austria, Italy, France, and Switzerland) and all of Europe's highest Alpine passes.

After collecting two Alpine Cups in the 1930 Austrian Alpine and the 1930 Alföld-Alpenfahrt, as well as winning the 1931 Monte outright, Donald Healey added the Glacier Cup of the 1931 International Alpine to his array of trophies for Invicta.

But out of these, only eight cars arrived with a clean sheet, all individual entries. They were Donald Healey (Invicta), Walter Delmár (Mercedes), and Desiderius von Bitzy (Austro-Daimler Bergmeister) in the unlimited class, as well as Count Felix Spiegel-Diesenberg (Austro-Daimler ADR), Philipp von Schoeller (Austro-Daimler ADR), Humfrey E Symons (Clément-Talbot), EAH Scholten (Lancia), and Carlo Adorno (OM) in the 3 litre class. Those eight drivers were awarded Glacier Cups. Three more of these, although "at a discount", were given to the three Hanomag drivers Hellmuth Butenuth, Carl Pollich, and Frau Liliane Roehrs who tied for a class win in the 1100cc class with 4 points each. Lord Clifford (MG Midget) put up a very creditable performance with only 13 penalty points, to receive a Silver Glacier Medal. Two years later, when he was in his mid-forties, Lord Clifford opted for the comfort of a Bentley and the fuel economy of a diesel engine for the 1933 Monte, and with this hybrid car he finished fifth overall. Other British finishers in the Alpine were WF Bradley (Armstrong-Siddeley), Victor E Leverett, AG Gripper (both Riley), and British-born Shelagh Brunner-Liechtenstein in her Austro-Daimler.

Although not a single car from the teams entered arrived without penalty, the German Wanderer and the Czech Praga-Piccolo Manufacturer's Team received Alpine Cups. In the 3 litre class it was Wanderer, with drivers Alexander Graumüller, Bernhard Bau, and Hans Hinterleitner, winning against the Belgian FN Team which also brought all three cars home. The Alpine Cup amongst the 1100s went to Praga-Piccolo (J Heussler, St Pavlovsky, and A Suldowsky), whilst only two out of the three Rileys made it to the finish.

For the 1932 event, a record number of 107 entries were received, and 99 cars actually started from Munich. Out of these, no less than 39 were British. The Germans were there in force as well, with 35 starters. There were also 7 Austrians, and smaller contingents from Czechoslovakia,

The Austrian steel magnate Philipp von Schoeller in his 3 litre ADR Austro-Daimler at Trafoi in the 1931 International Alpine.

A Pan-European effort 1928-1936

The Talbot Team with (l to r) the Hon Brian Lewis (later Lord Essendon), Tim Rose-Richards, and Norman Garrad (to become Sunbeam-Talbot team manager after WW II) won an International Alpine Cup in the over 2000cc unlimited class. By 1932 Britain fielded the strongest contingent with 39 participants; more than Germany's 35.

Switzerland, Italy, France, Holland and Hungary. The route passed through Austria into Italy (with a speed hill climb up the Stelvio where Donald Healey in the Invicta recorded fastest time of the day), Switzerland (San Bernardino hill climb), back into Italy, then to France, finally returning to San Remo on the Italian Riviera dei Fiori. 87 cars arrived at the finish and were greeted as heroes, particularly the 35 which came home with a clean sheet.

Of the seven teams entered, only two arrived at the finish without penalty, both teams competing in the over two litre unlimited class and claiming Alpine Cups of equal value. One of them was the Wanderer Team completely unchanged from the previous year (Graumüller, Bau, and Hinterleitner). The other one was the team of the invincible Talbots, with the Hon Brian Lewis (later to become Lord Essendon), TE 'Tim' Rose-Richards, and Norman Garrad, the latter to play an important role as team manager for Sunbeam-Talbot in the nineteen fifties. After the previous year's successful "Talbot recce" by *Sunday Times* correspondent HE Symons, this was the first official Talbot participation in an Alpine Trial. Georges Roesch as chief engineer was still responsible for the cars.

There were two more Coupes des Alpes for the winning – ie least penalized – teams in the 1500 and the 1100cc class: Tatra (Hans Schicht, Wolfgang von Mayenburg, and F Hoffmann) and Riley (Victor Leverett, Charles Riley, and G Dennison) got their cups at a reduced rate, so to speak.

Amongst the individual entrants competing for Glacier Cups the British swept the board. No fewer than 18 out of a total of 27 went to British cars and drivers. In the over 2 litre unlimited class there were three cups each for Invicta (Donald Healey, AG Lace, and Charles Needham) and Armstrong-Siddeley (CD Siddeley, HE Symons, and WF Bradley), whilst Tony Lago (Armstrong-Siddeley) and FW Morgan (Humber Super Snipe) collected some penalty marks, and the only Bentley (Home Kidston) retired. Continentals in this class took home 8 Glacier Cups, amongst them Hungarian Walter Delmár and German Rudi Sauerwein in their Bugattis. Wanderer and Ford drivers also won two cups each, and there was one Glacier Cup each for the Italian makes of Fiat (Dr Armand Lettich, Austria) and Lancia (EAH Scholten). There were only two cars in the 2 litre class which WM Couper (Lagonda) won from a Mercedes, thus collecting a Glacier Cup despite being penalized.

The 1500 class was completely dominated by the British, two Glacier Cups going to Wolseley and its remarkable lady drivers Katharine Martin and Margaret Allen (later to marry Christopher Jennings, editor of *The Motor*), and two more to Frazer Nash in its first attempt (Harold John Aldington and Archie Gripper). Amongst the three MGs that made it to the finish in the 1500cc class was 19 year old Cambridge undergraduate Dick Seaman, later of Grand Prix fame, in his 1250cc F-type Magna tourer, a present from his parents. He dropped a number of points, as did WE Belgrave. More successful was WEC Watkinson who won a Glacier Cup in his MG.

Five cups for Britain (Jack Hobbs, Roy Franey, GMD Maltby and C Montague-Johnstone in Rileys, Eric W Deeley in a Singer) against the sole cup for Dr Otto Enoch from Germany in his Hanomag – that was the 1100cc outcome. Other Rileys, a Singer, an MG, and a Triumph – on its maiden voyage to the Dolomites – with 1018cc Coventry Climax engine driven by Livingstone P Armstrong also finished, but collected penalty points.

At the summit of the Col di Lana, scene of the fiercest fighting between Italians and Austrians in the First World War, a control point was set up in 1933. AGR Alexander in Riley number 123 has just passed it to continue the difficult Dolomite stage.

In 1933 there were 132 entries from Austria, Belgium, Czechoslovakia, France, Germany, Great Britain (50 entries), Holland, Hungary, Italy, Switzerland, and the United States. At Merano in South Tyrol 121 cars were sent on their way to Nice, over a distance of 1193 miles. The first daily stage constituted

the 250 miles 'Dolomite Circuit' including the Pordoi Hill Climb. Here the British journalist WF Bradley scored fastest time of the day in his Hotchkiss. The third day practically commenced with the Stelvio Hill Climb where only seven drivers escaped penalties, the two Bugattis of Mademoiselle

A Pan-European effort 1928-1936

Hungarian Walter Delmár (Bugatti) was one of only three drivers to finish the 1933 International Alpine with a clean sheet. This earned him his third Glacier Cup, and a fourth was to follow in 1934. As a 20 year old Delmár finished the 1913 Austrian Alpine without loss of marks, and repeated this performance the following year.

Hellé Nice and Walter Delmár, the two Rileys of Jack Hobbs (1500) and Donald Healey (1100), as well as the Alfa Romeo of René Carrière, the MG of WE Belgrave, and the Frazer Nash of HJ Aldington. The route then lead into Switzerland with slightly easier going, while leg 4 brought the motorcade back into Italy and on to Torino. The last days were spent up and down the toughest French mountain passes including the dreaded and timed Col du Galibier with its fearfully unprotected edges. Just like the Stelvio, this was a key test in the Alpine Trial. It was almost impossible to maintain the prescribed speeds. Of the hitherto unpenalized seven, Belgrave dropped two points, while Mlle Hellé Nice, Donald Healey and Jack Hobbs were three points down. René Carrière in his supercharged Alfa Romeo put up fastest time of the day, and there were only three more drivers who got away without penalties, HJ Aldington

(Frazer Nash) as well as the two Bugattis of Walter Delmár and Edouard Legré, but the latter had picked up one point at the Stelvio. Thus, Carrière, Delmár and Aldington were the only ones to arrive at the finish in Nice with a clean sheet. Mlle Hellé-Nice, a danseuse from the Casino de Paris with the real name of Hélène Delangle, was a mere three points down, the highest placed lady driver in the 1933 International Alpine. However, as she preferred male company also in a Trial (in this case Monsieur Bonnet) she did not receive the Coupe des Dames reserved for "equipages exclusivement féminins". Instead, it went to Miss Dorothy Champney/Miss L Hobbs, 56 points down in their Riley. Out of 121 starters, 95 arrived in Nice and were classified, only three of them with a clean sheet. This was due to the very stiff standard times in the Stelvio and Galibier hill climbs rather than the car-breaking character of the event.

Of all the 16 teams competing for Manufacturers' Team Awards and Alpine Cups, and comprising 48 competitors, there was but one man who made it, HJ Aldington. Proud of his 1932 Glacier Cup, the boss of Frazer Nash saw to it that no less than eight of his cars took part in the Trial, three (including himself) competing as a Manufacturer's Team, and five more individual entries out to get Glacier Cups. Much to his regret the other two team cars were laden with 99 penalty points, so the Frazer Nash Team was only second to the Riley Team in the 1500 class. Thus, no Coupe des Alpes for Frazer Nash, and no Glacier Cup for Aldington. As a team member he was ineligible for that trophy. There were five Alpine Cups for the Teams least penalized in each class: 1100cc: MG (Tommy Wisdom, WEC Watkinson, and LA Welch); 1500cc: Riley (C Riley, J Ridley, TC Griffiths); 2000cc: Adler (F Widenmann, Plilipp Hoffmann, A Gehrmann); 3000cc: Hotchkiss (WF Bradley, Duhamel and Gas, with a total of 36 points the least penalized team of them all); and unlimited: Ford of Holland (N Went, Dr JJ Sprenger van Eyk, AAJ Wieleman).

In their capacity as individual entrants Carrière (Alfa Romeo) and Delmár (Bugatti), the other two drivers without penalties, were more fortunate than Aldington, insofar as they were rewarded with Coupes des Glaciers. For René Carrière and his co-driver Henry Avril, both from Marseilles, the Alpes Maritimes were familiar hunting grounds, and his class win in the first ever Rallye des Alpes Françaises of 1932 certainly

The Coming Out Party of the Jaguar-forerunner SS 1 in the 1933 International Alpine Trial witnessed a disaster for the works team, but the situation was saved by the Austrian Standard concessionnaire Hans Georg Koch (no. 38) who was best SS1 driver right behind a bunch of powerful Bugattis in the three litre class. Count Peter Orssich in the SS 1 Coupé with smaller engine (no. 39) also made it to the finish. Edouard Legré's Bugatti (no. 36) can be seen in the background on the right; he lost only a single point.

Having won a Glacier Cup in 1932 (see colour painting on front cover) HJ Aldington fielded a team of three Frazer Nashes with Adrian Thorpe (no. 84), Lionel Butler-Henderson (no. 85) and HJ Aldington (no. 86). The latter was the only team driver (out of 48) to finish the trial with a clean sheet.

had been good training. In the forties Avril, and in the early fifties Carrière, then acted as Clerk of the Course of the French Alpine Rally. Forty-year old Hungarian ace Walter Delmár in his Bugatti, 3 litre class winner, added a third Glacier Cup to his collection of 1931 (Mercedes) and 1932 (Bugatti). His first Alpine experience dated back to 1913 when he completed the Austrian Alpenfahrt without loss of marks in a Benz, at the tender age of twenty, repeating the achievement in 1914. In the twenties he raced Steyr cars in continental hill climbs with great success.

Those individual entrants winning their class with penalty points also received Glacier Cups, at a discount. They were WE Belgrave (MG, 1100, -2), Jack Hobbs (Riley, 1500, -3) as well as the two Dutchmen Jacques van der Meulen and van Beek Calkoen who tied for the unlimited class win in their Fords, 7 points down each. The 1933 Alpine Trial also marked the continental competitions debut for William Lyons' new Swallow SS 1. The three works cars (Tourers) encountered endless technical troubles, and only Charles Needham reached the finish line, 8th in the 3 litre class. It was fortunate for this Jaguar forerunner that there were also two Austrian entries.

Hans Georg Koch, the Austrian Swallow concessionnaire, drove a British-registered SS 1 Tourer into 6th place in the 3 litre class (behind four Bugattis led by Delmár, and a Hotchkiss), while Count Peter Orssich/Ernst von Stahl was 11th in his own SS 1 Coupé. with Austrian registration plates. Koch remained faithful to William Lyons as Austrian Jaguar importer till his dying day. Then, in the late sixties, his widow had to make way for British Leyland's Austrian subsidiary.

The theme of the 1934 Coupe Internationale des Alpes was Nice to Munich via Zagreb, a very ambitious proposition extending the total distance to more than 1800 miles. The trial commenced with considerable route changes and detours in the French Alps due to a major landslide which eliminated the timed Galibier Hill Climb. The second and third daily stages covered Switzerland where the required average speeds

The Wanderer of Johann Hinterleitner in one of the many Stelvio hairpin bends (1934). Both in 1931 and 1932 Hinterleitner was a member of the Alpine Cup winning Wanderer team.

were massively reduced. The route then passed into Italy via the Stelvio Hill Climb but without further difficulties. To complement the speed hill climbs, the Italians, proud of their new Autostrada, also organized a five kilometre speed test. The fifth day took the cars to an Alpine area last tackled in the pre-Kaiser War 'Alpenfahrt'. From Venice to Zagreb in Yugoslavia it was a high speed procession on main roads, although the country had more mountainous alternatives to offer. But then the route turned north-west into Austria via Wurzenpass and led to Turracher Höhe. There, the Singer 9s successfully mastered its gradient of 1 in 3, but only in reverse gear! From then on it was easier going to the finish at Munich.

In the light of 1933 results the time schedules had been eased considerably. A record number of 127 cars had started in Nice, and no less than 94 of them finished the sixth and last daily stage from Zagreb to Munich. The unusually large number of cars (56) finished without loss of marks. Of the 15 participating three-car Manufacturers' Teams, eight would claim Alpine Cups. All in all 35 Glacier Cups were distributed to individual entrants.

In the over 3 litre unlimited class the old-established Delahaye Company made a renewed effort to re-establish itself as a prestigious make of sporting character. At the 1933 Paris Show two new models had been introduced, the type 124 12CV

In 1934 Opel won an Alpine Cup (Team Award) and two Glacier Cups, one of those for Edith Frisch who is seen here leading TC Griffiths in a Riley. Griffiths had been a member of the winning Riley Team in 1933.

four cylinder, and the type 134 18CV six cylinder. Then, at the request of millionairesse Lucy O'Reilly-Schell, Delahaye chief engineer Charles Weiffenbach fitted the 110bhp 3227cc six into the smaller type 124 chassis, and four of these cars were entered for the 1934 Alpine Trial. The cars did very well against an armada of 17 Ford V8s that traditionally dominated the over 3 litre class. The Delahaye Team (Albert Perrot, Marcel Dhôme, and Robert Girod) won the Alpine Cup, although Perrot retired which cost 300 points, thus leaving the trouble-ridden Dutch

Ford Team (Jacques van der Meulen, van Beek Calkoen and G Bakker-Schut) behind. Individual entrants saved Ford's honour by winning six Glacier Cups, as against one for the Delahaye driven by Mrs Lucy Schell-O'Reilly/Laury Schell. There were five more Glacier Cups in the unlimited class, for the two 3.3 litre Bugattis of Gaston Descollas and von Biro, for the two new Railton Terraplanes of RL Richardson and DH Davids, and for the big Hotchkiss of Jean Trevoux.

Amongst the 3 litres all three Talbot 105s (Tommy

Wisdom, WM Couper and Hugh Eaton) entered by the London concessionnaire Charlie Joyce came home without loss of points as an intact team to score an Alpine Cup. But sadly, Talbot was in serious financial trouble, and was soon broken up. The case of the three German Adler Diplomat cars (Günther Wimmer, Adolf Max Gehrmann and Philipp Hoffmann) was not so clear cut. The team was first announced as an unpenalized Alpine Cup winner, but in the printed results all three cars had disappeared from the list, only to gloriously reappear as Coupe des Alpes winners in the officially printed year-end report. This indicates a protest and a consequent decision by the Court of Appeal. As in the year before, Swallow was also competing for the 3 litre Team Award with three SS 1 Tourers. Both Charles Needham and Douglas Clease were well placed but Sydney Light retired after a crash, but still the effort was rewarded with a gold-plated silver medal (second class award). FW Morgan gained a second class award driving a similar car as an individual entrant. The only Glacier Cup in this class went to René Carrière/Henry Avril, this time driving a Hotchkiss.

In the 2 litre class no less than three Coupes des Alpes were distributed. The Adler Trumpf Team consisted of Paul von Guilleaume, Rudolf Hasse, and Otto Löhr. Rudolph Sauerwein and Walter Delmár in their individually entered Adler Super Trumpf models won Coupes des Glaciers. For the Hungarian this was his fourth consecutive Glacier Cup! Wanderer fielded two teams of its new W 22 model, one composed of 1931 and 1932 Cup winners Graumüller, Hinterleitner, and Bau, the other one consisting of Count Max Sandizell, Karl Friedrich Trübsbach, and Willi Kraemer. While the first team had to make do with a Silver Medal (third class award), it was the less experienced second team which brought home the Coupe des Alpes. The third Alpine Cup went to the new Opel sports two seaters driven by Heinrich Diehl, Alex Blüm, and Franz Traiser. There were also two Glacier Cups for the individual Opel entrants Miss Edith Frisch and Willy Engesser. The Riley Team amongst the 2 litres (Charles Riley, A Farrar, and TC Griffiths) won a second class award, 'la plaquette en vermeil', a gold-plated silver medal. And finally there was a Glacier Cup for von Goldegg, from Czechoslovakia, in his Alfa Romeo.

BMW entered a team of three of its latest type 315/1 sports cars with 40bhp six cylinder engine. They were driven by

Richard Brenner/Werberger, Albert Kandt/Koch, and Ernst von Delius/Leidenberger. This team came home to Munich without loss of marks, thus winning the only Alpine Cup in the 1500cc class. Two similar cars driven by Count Felix Spiegel zum Diesenberg and Frau Roehrs won Glacier Cups. BMW's most serious competitor in the 1500 class was Frazer Nash with its team composed of Lionel Butler-Henderson, Alan Marshall, and the Hon Peter Mitchell-Thomson. The first two had clean sheets but Mitchell-Thomson dropped 14 points, thus giving the Alpine Cup to BMW. There were also three individual Frazer Nash entries, of HJ Aldington, John Tweedale, and Mrs Arlene Needham. For the third consecutive year Aldy arrived without loss of marks. He and Tweedale received Glacier Cups but poor Mrs Needham had the hard luck of losing one single point. Aldington was deeply impressed by the more modern BMW 315 which, with its superior roadholding, could outperform the Frazer Nash uphill or downhill. This was a good reason for entering into negotiations with the Munich-based works. Soon an agreement was reached whereby Frazer Nash

The new BMW 315/1 sports car. Richard Brenner, Albert Kandt Jr and Ernst von Delius formed the BMW Team that won the Coupe des Alpes of the 1500cc class. The new type 315/1, with its 1500cc six cylinder engine, impressed everybody, and HJ Aldington was quick to make a deal with the Bavarians to market the 'Frazer Nash-BMW' in Britain.

was to sell BMWs in Great Britain under the name of Frazer Nash-BMW. There were seven more Coupes des Glaciers for individual entries in the 1½ litre class, two Aston Martins driven by chocolate king Peter Cadbury and T Clarke, two Röhr cars (Arthur von Mumm and Alfred Gutknecht), one MG Magnette (HE Symons), one Standard Avon (Count Peter Orssich), and Capt OH Frost's Lancia Augusta.

Which brings us to the 1100cc class where three teams competed. Frau Lotte Bahr, A Kronmüller and FK Widenmann represented Adler with its smallest Junior model, and Singer had lined up WJB Richardson, AH Langley, and HM Avery. But it was the Triumph Team of three 972cc SX Tens (LtCol Claude Vivian Holbrook, JC Ridley, and Victor E Leverett) that won the 1100cc Alpine Cup, and this success was complemented by Glacier Cups for the individual entries of Donald Healey and MA Newnham. The Singer Team was second, and Adler third, Widenmann retiring at Turracher Höhe. There was no reason for Singer to be discontented, as three Glacier Cups also came its way, procured by RP Gardner, FS Barnes, and IF Connell. Paul Schweder won a Coupe des Glaciers in his own Adler Junior.

Cars and components were submitted to such extraordinary stress in these Alpine Trials that such mountainous reliability tests over long distances were not only considered a sport, they were also seen as most valuable technical tests. This was particularly true in the thirties in its delicate and difficult political and economic climate. Countries without indigenous oil resources were frantically trying to become less dependent on oil and petrol imports. The Austrian Economic Board (Österreichisches Kuratorium für Wirtschaftlichkeit) took the initiative and proposed a special Alpine Trial to test the Ersatz fuels for internal combustion engines. The Swiss Society for the Study of Engine Fuels and the National Fascist Association of the Motor Industry in Italy joined in, as did four Austrian Ministries and the National Automobile Clubs of those three countries. From 22nd September to 4th October 1934 the 'First International Alpine Trial for Motor Cars with Ersatz Fuel' was run over a distance of 2000 kilometres in Austria, Switzerland and Italy, starting and finishing at Innsbruck. Wood gas, charcoal gas, 'Corethstoff', methanol, and distillate of lignite tar were tested in cars and lorries as substitutes for petrol. It is remarkable that Germany

in its search for self-sufficiency did not participate, but following the assassination of the Austrian Federal Chancellor Dr Engelbert Dollfuss by the Nazis, relations between Austria and Germany were very tense indeed.

Two years later, in 1936, the Swiss Society for the Study of Engine Fuels held the 2nd International Alpine Trial for Motor Cars with Ersatz Fuel. It started (and finished) in Berne, and was run only on Swiss territory over a distance of 2000 kilometres. This time cars were not involved, the event concentrated on commercial vehicles. The Swiss motor industry, the Austrian Army and both the Swiss and Austrian Mail participated. All this might seem ludicrous today but those who lived through World War II on the continent of Europe still recall those cars and lorries converted to wood gas. They were the only ones seen on the road, as petrol was reserved for the German Army.

International cooperation fizzled out, however, as the political tension mounted in Europe. The 1935 Alpine was scheduled to start in Munich, with hill climbs on the Stelvio and the Galibier, as well as a 100 kilometre speed test on the Milan-Torino Autostrada. There, supercharged cars would have to average no less than 75mph (120kph), and 53mph (85kph) was prescribed for the 1100cc class. Aix-les Bains was selected as the final destination, but all this was not to be. Italy was preparing for the Abyssinian War and, therefore, was threatened with sanctions by the League of Nations. Also, Nazi Germany, short of foreign currency, blocked the transfer of all German entry fees, for a total of 74 cars. So, much to everyone's regret the Automobile Club de France cancelled the 1935 event.

The VIII – and last – International Alpine Trial of 1936 run by the Swiss Club was but a shadow of its forerunners. Under sanctions Italy abstained, whilst the Automobile Clubs of Austria, France, Germany, and Great Britain remained as nominal co-organizers. The 1455 mile event was run on Swiss territory and at ridiculously low average speeds. 72 cars started in Lucerne, 64 finished, 23 of them with a clean sheet. There were three speed hill climbs (Klausenpass, Bernina, and Weissenstein near Solothurn), plus a 'kilomètre lancé' speed test near St Moritz. In the speed test, fastest time of the day went to Gaston Descollas (Bugatti 3.3 litre, 26.1sec), while the new 2.5 litre Jaguar SS 100, in the hands of Tommy and Elsie

The 1936 International Alpine saw the first resounding international success of the new Jaguar SS 100, driven by Tommy and Elsie Wisdom, shown here at a stop near Neuchatel.

Paul von Guilleaume at the Col de Pillon in Switzerland, driving one of the Adler Trumpf Team cars that won a 1936 Coupe des Alpes, bringing the total for Adler teams to an unrivalled five. Adler's success in trials was above all the result of excellent road holding, not its conventional side valve engines.

The DKW Team car of Wilhelm Kraemer/Otto Munzert (no. 62) leads the private DKW of Count Bassewitz (no. 63) in the 1936 International Alpine Trial. The Team won an Alpine Cup, and there were four Glacier Cups for individual DKW entries.

Wisdom was not much slower (26.8sec) and fastest 3 litre. Alfred Gutknecht, BMW, (28.7sec) scored best amongst the 2 litre cars, and Dr Siebert (DKW, 34.8 sec) was fastest 1100.

Manufacturers Teams again competed for Alpine Cups, and four of these were awarded in their respective cubic capacity classes, to DKW, Adler, Hanomag and Ford. The DKWs (Fritz Trägner, Alfred Weidauer, Willi Kraemer) were the only team to bring home their full contingent of 3000 points, while Ford (Lex van Strien, Karel Ton, Jan Erens), Adler (Paul von Guilleaume, Rudi Sauerwein, Count Peter Orssich) and Hanomag (Karl Haeberle, W Glöckler, G Roericht) all suffered some loss of points. Three individual entrants in the unlimited class received Glacier Cups, one Lincoln and two Fords, while Descollas lost a few points which meant a second class award, just like HE Symons (Wolseley) and WG Lockhart (Bentley). There were three Coupes des Glaciers for the 3 litre cars, the Wisdom couple, Swiss driver Oskar Bally (Talbot) and G Wimmer in a big Adler. Donald Healey (Triumph) won his fourth Glacier Cup, while the six other 2 litre Cups all went to BMW drivers (Baron CA Aretin, Baron Günther Egloffstein, Alfred Gutknecht, Friedrich Holzhäuer, H Meffert and A Schmidt), an outstanding achievement. And finally, there were four Glacier Cups in the 1100 class, all going to DKWs. And as the cars reached the finish line at Interlaken, it was time to close the book of the once glorious International Alpine Trials ...

The gathering storm

When no International Alpine Trial was held in 1937, the Austrian Automobile Club took the chance to run a proper Austrian Alpine Trial, with the hope of picking up the heirloom, and to become its successor. In the years 1933 through 1935, the club had organized minor Austrian Alpine Cup Trials (or Höhenstrassenfahrten as some of them were also called), mainly for domestic consumption, and of little international importance. Now, the start and finish of this 1860km (1155 mile) event was the spa resort of Baden, near Vienna, and there were five special tests. A retirement quota of 50% indicated its ambitious character. Participation was part local, part German. With the disappearance of Austro-Daimler through the merger with Steyr, the country no longer produced sports cars of high performance. The result was a walkover for the modern new sports cars from Germany. Hanomag took the first two places in general classification (Fritz Huschke von Hanstein and Frau Christl Meinecke), and the Opel of Carl von Guilleaume was

third. BMW had to be content with an ex-aequo two litre class win for Count Heinrich von der Mühle, while the Austrian C Peter Blaimschein won the 1100cc class in his Fiat Balilla.

Preparations for another Austrian Alpine Trial were under way the following year, but then the whole country underwent a trial of a different kind. On February 12th 1938 the Austrian Federal Chancellor, Dr Kurt von Schuschnigg, had a meeting with Adolf Hitler at Berchtesgaden. Bullied by threats and the presence of numerous German Generals he agreed to appoint some Nazi ministers to his cabinet. Yet upon return to Vienna he had second thoughts and called a plebiscite "for a free and independent Austria" to be held on March 13th. Left alone by Italy and the Western Powers he finally gave in to Hitler's military threats and resigned. On March 12th the Wehrmacht marched into Austria, which became part of Germany. There was no military resistance.

The Austrian Automobile Club was immediately dissolved, to be succeeded by 'Der Deutsche Automobil Club' (DDAC) and Nationalsozialistisches Kraftfahr-Korps (NSKK). The Austrian Alpine Trial was renamed 'Deutsche Alpenfahrt', and run under the leadership of NSKK Gruppenführer Kurt von Barisani. Private entries were a thing of the past, each participant started for the organization to which he belonged: Wehrmacht, SS, NSKK, Reichspost or DDAC, an organization without party membership requirement.

Deutsche Alpenfahrt started at Innsbruck and finished in Vienna. The highest awards were Alpine Cups, one for Sports Cars and one for Production Touring Cars. Class winners received a Silver Edelweiss, and everyone with a clean sheet got a Gold Medal. There were heaps of them, as the event was not particularly testing. All but one class win went to German makes, such was the domination of the German motor industry. It was announced that the Alpine Cup for Touring Cars went to the excellent German driver Bobby Kohlrausch (Opel) who had successfully driven the 'Mighty Midget' MG on the continent in the mid-thirties. Class winners were W Kramer (NSU-Fiat, 1100cc), Kohlrausch (Opel, 1500cc), and Alois Zimmermann (Alfa Romeo, unlimited).

Amongst the Sports Cars, it was Fritz Trägner (DKW, 1100cc), Eugen Krings (BMW, 1500cc), Fritz Roth (BMW, 2000cc), Franz Lucas (Mercedes, 3000cc), and Sporn (Stoewer, over 3000cc unlimited), the Alpine Cup going to

Fritz Roth in his BMW 328 was hard to beat in the last Trials before the outbreak of the war. Winning the German Alpine Cup for sports cars in 1938 (picture, at Grossglockner) as well as 1939, he also scored fastest time of the day at the Miramas Circuit in the 1939 French Alpine.

Fritz Roth in his BMW 328. Also, there were three Team Awards, two of them for Adam Opel AG with drivers Carl von Guilleaume, Heiner Vogt and Kohlrausch as well as Fritz Göbel, Hermann Bernhard and Heinrich Diehl. Ford was the third team to claim an award for drivers Erich Pätzold, Alfons Ostermann and Walter Scheube. Yet the team had not been entered under the name of Ford, but as NSKK-Motorgruppe Niederrhein!

The organization of the event, particularly on the road, reflected German precision and perfection. Yet the day after the prize-giving, held on the steps of the Vienna City Hall by

NSKK-Korpsführer Adolf Hühnlein himself, the press office had to admit some errors in the points calculation. Thus, the touring car Alpine Cup did not go to Bobby Kohlrausch, but to another Opel driven by Edgar Kittner ...

There was another Deutsche Alpenfahrt in 1939, from 31st July through 2nd August. The avoidance of understatements in a preview published in *Neues Wiener Tagblatt* is symptomatic for the controlled press in those days: "The most difficult and interesting long distance test in Europe's motor sport will be, like last year, the Deutsche Alpenfahrt, this time inscribed by the ONS in the International Calendar. This year the start will no longer be at Innsbruck but in Munich. Vienna as the second City of Grossdeutsches Reich will again be the final destination of the event".

The Trial included 34 Alpine Passes over a distance of 1000 miles and was a bit more testing than the year before. 104 sports cars and 37 production touring cars started in Munich, with hardly any participants from abroad. The itinerary lead over Kesselberg to Innsbruck and further via Grossglockner to the finish of the first daily stage in Villach. The second day was tougher, over such dreaded mountain passes as Turracher Höhe (special stage) and. Katschberg. At Wurzenpass the cars entered Yugoslavia which they left after a short 40 mile stretch via Loibl pass. At the end of this day the cavalcade arrived at Semmering, site of an old traditional hill climb first held in 1899. The third stage finally led to the finish in Vienna.

Both touring car classes – up to 1500 and 3000cc – went to Opels, driven by Kittner (Olympia) and Diehl (Kapitän), both well known from last year. And it was Edgar Kittner again to take home the Alpine Cup for Touring cars. Fritz Roth (BMW 328), last year's sports car winner, once more claimed the Sports Car Alpine Cup, also winning the 2 litre class, of course. Herbert Ahrem (BMW) won the 1500cc, and Toni Magnus (Mercedes) the 3 litre sports car class.

The 1939 Deutsche Alpenfahrt was also quite an important Motor Cycle Trial. The over 350cc unlimited class was won by Wolfgang Denzel, riding a BMW. He was duly rewarded with an Alpine Cup, the second one he had won inside of a fortnight. The previous one he collected at Marseilles, driving a BMW 328 in the Rallye des Alpes Françaises, yet another pretender for the spiritual heirloom of the International Alpine Trial, as we shall see in the next chapter.

France takes over 1938–1971

As the International Alpine Trial unfolded and the Automobile Club de France decided to join the four founder members (Italy, Germany, Austria, and Switzerland), it delegated Albert Rousset, President of the Automobile Club de Marseille et Provence, to the 1931 International Alpine. Rousset asked Edouard Legré to accompany him, and both were deeply impressed by what they saw, particularly in the Austrian section. As a consequence they decided to organize the Rallye des Alpes Françaises, initially an event for domestic consumption. It was first held in 1932 and completely ignored cubic capacity classes as used in motor sport worldwide. Instead, there were classes based on French retail prices. Thus, cars were grouped up to frs 30,000-, 40,000-, 50,000- and above. The most expensive class in the initial event saw the Alfa Romeo of René Carrière victorious. In 1933 we note that the dearest class went to Legré's Bugatti, while the cheapest – up to 20,000 French francs – was won by an Amilcar driven by a Frenchman named Gaston Descollas. In 1934 he was back in a Bugatti with which he won the over frs 70,000- unlimited class.

By 1935 the organizers had had second thoughts about the validity of price classes, so invented a coefficient based on price and cubic capacity. Again, Descollas was successful with his new Type 57 Bugatti, winning the highest coefficient class. The next class went to Albert Perrot (Delahaye), and it was the duel for fastest time of the day in the Galibier and Mont Ventoux Hill Climbs of Descollas versus Perrot that made the event so exciting. However, there was still general unhappiness with this enigmatic formula, so cubic capacity classes – up to 1500, 3000, and over 3000cc – were introduced for the French Alpine Rally of 1936, more in line with the growing ambitions of the Club. Henry Avril stepped in to become Clerk of the Course, replacing René Larroque. Guy Lapchin (Riley) won the smallest class, Pfister (Citroën) the intermediate one, and

The 1938 French Alpine was the first one open to foreign competitors and offered a Coupe des Alpes for all those arriving without loss of marks. Shown here is the winning BMW 328 of Bavarian Count Heinrich von der Mühle, with Germany's most attractive co-driver, Eugenie von Plessen, standing by the car.

Gaston and Claire Descollas first made the headlines when they won the 1935 Critérium Paris-Nice in their new Type 57 Bugatti. All in all, between 1934 and 1948 this extraordinary couple won one Glacier Cup and four Coupes des Alpes, driving for Amilcar, Bugatti, and Lancia. The Bugatti was recently restored by Hero Alting, of Osnabrück.

France takes over 1938-1971

Carrière was victorious amongst the big ones, this time driving a Matford, a Ford V8 assembled by Mathis for the French market. However, in order to cater for the French amateurs, Alpine Trophies went to the winners of classes up to and over frs. 20.000.-, both won by Renault cars.

No Rallye des Alpes Françaises was held in 1937, a year marred by troubles in France and the Spanish Civil War. However, in that fateful year, André Baron d'Huart Saint Mauris was elected President of the Automobile Club de Marseille et Provence. With the demise of the International Coupe des Alpes he saw a tremendous opportunity for 1938. He had the vision and the energy to turn the French Alpine into a major international event, and he stood at the helm of the Club for more than two decades, during the heydays of the French Alpine. To establish a claim to the heritage of the International Alpine Trials his Rallye des Alpes Françaises of 1938 was stiffened beyond recognition, and inscribed in the International Calendar to attract foreign participants. A Coupe des Alpes was offered to all those who came home with a clean sheet, and only two drivers achieved this almost impossible task. The Bavarian Count Heinrich von der Mühle put up fastest time of the day in all the special tests (including a lap of the Miramas Circuit) with his BMW 328 and finished without any loss of points. In a letter to the author the 94 year old gentleman, last surviving participant of pre-war Alpines, described the event: "The French Alpine was run over narrow untarred roads in the French Alps. Hairpins were so narrow that one had to reverse to get round. In addition every day there was a hill climb over distances of 12 to 42 kilometres, and then the circuit race in Marseilles (Miramas). I put up fastest time in all the special tests and came back with nine cups of genuine silver."

Not surprisingly, the other of the two Cups went to the Bugatti and Lancia dealer in Marseilles, Gaston Descollas, this time driving a Lancia Aprilia. He already had a 1934 Glacier Cup to his credit, and had scored class wins in no less than three of the five French Alpine Rallies held until then.

Count von der Mühle's success raised interest for this rally in Germany. His sister was married to another BMW driver of repute, Baron Alexander von Falkenhausen, whose name will creep up in this narrative time and again. It was he who instigated a strong BMW participation for the 1939 event which was at least as tough. These 328s were driven

Wolfgang Denzel won one of the two Coupes des Alpes in the 1939 event, driving a BMW 328, no. 36 (no. 28 Roth, no. 31 von Falkenhausen). Like the previous year, the second Coupe des Alpes went to a Lancia Aprilia, but this time its driver was not Gaston Descollas, but his wife Claire.

by von Falkenhausen, Rudi Sauerwein, Fritz Roth, Dr Peter Wessely, and a crack motorcycle rider from Graz, formerly in Austria, a country that had disappeared from the map the previous year to form part of Grossdeutschland. His name was Wolfgang Denzel, and it was his first competition outing on four wheels. He came from a family of bell founders but had entered the motor business and was BMW concessionnaire in Graz. The rally commenced with a wiggle-woggle test at Aix-les Bains which was won by a Briton with the outlandish name of Tirachini in an SS Jaguar, but from that moment the continentals had it all their way. Seven drivers still held a clean sheet at the start of the third daily stage from Grenoble to Marseilles which was spiced with Galibier, Izoard and Col du Vars. Only two of these seven made it to Barcelonnette without loss of points, and from there to the Miramas circuit race it was easy going. At Miramas, Fritz Roth (BMW) was outright fastest, but no longer in the running for a Coupe des Alpes. As in the previous year there were only two Cups, and the happy winners were Wolfgang Denzel in a BMW 328, and Mme Claire Descollas in a Lancia Aprilia, a result reminiscent of 1938. The Cup winners also won the 2000 and 1500cc classes, the four remaining ones going to French drivers in French cars: A Montana (Matford), C de Cortanze (Peugeot 402), Gallo (Simca 8) and Michel Réal (Simca 5). A fortnight later Denzel mounted a BMW motorcycle to win another Alpine Cup, this time on two wheels and in 'Deutsche Alpenfahrt', as told in a previous chapter.

Towards the Golden Years

No country in Europe was as quick as France to resume motor sport after VE Day, the end of hostilities in Europe. In the Bois de Boulogne the first postwar motor race was held on September 9th 1945, and the French Alpine Rally was back in the calendar for 1946. The 37 starters all used pre-war cars, of course, and no one could claim a Coupe des Alpes as all the 13 cars at the finish had collected penalty points. Two of them were excluded for exceeding the time limit. Fastest in the standing start kilometre was Daligand (Bugatti, 34.2sec) who later retired. Robert Manzon, soon to become a Grand Prix driver, won the 1100 class in a Simca 8 with only 100 penalty points, the best result overall. Miss Betty Haig (AC 2 litre) won

In 1948, however, it was still possible to win a Coupe des Alpes in a ten year old pre-war car. Ian Appleyard/Dr Richard Weatherhead drove an SS 100 Jaguar fitted with a slightly younger 3.5 litre ohv engine.

Inclusion of the Dolomite Circuit in Italy set new standards in the 1949 French Alpine. Gaston Gautruche in his Citroën 11 was the only driver to come back with a clean sheet. A Coupe des Alpes and a kiss from Mme Odette Avril, wife of the Clerk of the Course, was his reward.

her class and the Coupe des Dames. Two class wins went to French Hotchkiss cars, R Huguet winning the unlimited class in a 3.5 litre 20CV (followed by Maurice Gatsonides in his

In 1948 the French Alpine ventured across the border for the first time to include a leg in Switzerland. This neutral island of wealth offered beautifully maintained mountain roads, unknown in the rest of Europe after the end of the war. Here, Tommy Wisdom, in a brand new Sunbeam-Talbot 90, drives up the St Gotthard Pass, but it was his Scots team-mate, George Murray-Frame, who won an Alpine Cup and the two litre class.

Gatford), and Bléin the three litre class in a smaller model. Simca, the French Fiat derivative, also won the Team Prize and scored yet another class win: Dr Marc Angelvin and his wife Nicole in their Simca 5 (Topolino) were best amongst the 750cc cars.

The event was acclaimed a great success, and the following year there was a stronger contingent from Britain to

rival the domestic heroes. This time, there was a Coupe des Alpes for Gaston Descollas who had distinguished himself so often before the war, driving a 2.3 litre Type 43 Bugatti, and winning the 'Compresseur' class. André Clermont brought a Lancia Aprilia home with a clean sheet to win the only other Coupe des Alpes, as well as the 1500cc class ahead of Mimi Descollas in a similar car. Again, there was a British class win

(3000cc), this time for Tommy Wisdom driving a Silverstone Healey. French cars also chalked up four more class wins: Dolf Burgerhout (Delahaye 135, unlimited), Jean Sandt (Citroën, 2000), Pierre Gay (Simca, 1100), and Mme Nicole Angelvin (Simca, 750) who this time seems to have signed the entry form instead of her husband. Third in the unlimited class was a nine year old Jaguar SS 100 with 3½ litre ohv engine driven by 23 year old Ian Appleyard. The Team Prize went to Simca.

Whilst the first two postwar editions of the rally were run inside France, 1948 marked the first venture across the border – into Switzerland. 71 cars started in Marseilles, to tackle a distance of 1167 miles. The first leg included a regularity test up Mont Ventoux, the second led into Switzerland, and on the fourth day the cars returned to France. British cars dominated the Col d'Izoard Hill Climb where Ian Appleyard in his Jaguar SS 100 was fastest, with Len Potter (Allard) only 1.6 seconds behind. Donald Healey in a Silverstone Healey was third, followed by the two Lancia Aprilias of Monsieur and Madame Gaston Descollas and the French Team Claude/Clause. Maximum permissible times for the Izoard were difficult to meet, and only 11 cars passed this test without penalty. On to the finish at Nice, where 29 cars arrived and were classified. The number of British and French entries were about equal, and the top honours were fairly shared. Eight cars were awarded Coupes des Alpes for arriving with a clean sheet, four of them going to British and four to French competitors.

Jaguar (Ian Appleyard/Dr Dick Weatherhead, class winners over 3000 unlimited), Allard (Leonard Potter), Sunbeam-Talbot 90 (George Murray-Frame, class win, 2000), and HRG (Robin Richards, class win, 1100) were the British makes ennobled by Alpine Cups. Amongst the French Cup winners was Gaston Descollas, almost as a matter of course, but this time he once again put his trust in an Italian Lancia Aprilia (as did Claude who had an overall win in the 1947 Mont Ventoux Hill Climb to his credit). This left only two Coupes des Alpes for French makes, one for the Citroën traction avant of Gaston Gautruche (second behind Murray-Frame in the 2000 class) and Freddy Auriach in a Simca 8 (second behind the HRG in the 1100 class). Whilst missing a Coupe des Alpes, Donald Healey won the three litre class in his Silverstone Healey. The one make team prize went to HRG (Robin Richards, Jack Richmond, and JHG Gott).

In 1950 the new ultra-light Dyna Panhard with 610cc air cooled engine set new standards, and thereby upset the handicap balance. Shown here is Dutchman Dolf Burgerhout in his Dyna no. 9. Six out of the seven Coupes des Alpes awarded went to these new French minicars.

All this encouraged the British community to give the Alpine a high priority. In 1949, 53 out of the 92 starters were British. Spurred by Murray-Frame's success in the newly designed Sunbeam-Talbot 90, the Rootes Group sent no less than four of these sporting saloons to Marseilles. The organizers clearly signalled their ambition to turn the rally into a true successor of the inter-war International Alpine Trials by including not only Switzerland, but also an important Italian section, increasing the distance to 1830 miles. They were rewarded by entries from 11 nations, more than double the 1948 figure. This Alpine Rally turned out to be an extra tough event, above all due to the integration of the Dolomite Circuit closed to other traffic. It was also used for the Coppa d'Oro delle Dolomiti Road Race the day after the rally passed through. Only one man finished this gruelling section without penalty, which included the

Pat Lyons, the daughter of Jaguar's founding father, married Ian Appleyard in spring 1950 and spent a sort of extended honeymoon in the French Alpine, driving the new light alloy XK 120 to victory – and the seventh Coupe des Alpes of that year.

Healey (Healey), two more Allards and HJ Aldington who had returned to the Alpine after 15 years. He drove one of the four two litre Bristol 400s, the first model designed by the British Aeroplane Company.

Upon arrival in Nice Gautruche received the only Coupe des Alpes awarded that year. He won the two litre class, and Citroën also took the Manufacturers' Team Prize (Gautruche, Andrew Black and Greek driver André Gerakis), while the three Sunbeams of Norman Garrad, Peter Monkhouse, and AG Douglas Clease received the award for the best non-French make. The other class winners were Len Potter (Allard, who also scored fastest time of the day at the Stelvio), Donald Healey/Ian Appleyard (Silverstone Healey), Betty Haig (MG TC, also winning the Coupe des Dames), Yves Lesur (Simca 8), and Ivan Hodač from Czechoslovakia in a 750cc Aero Minor with two cylinder two stroke engine.

In 1950 Henry Avril, who had been the competent Clerk of the Course for five years, handed over to his old partner in the 1933 International Alpine, René Carrière. The addition of Austria with its Grossglockner Pass made the French Alpine even more international, and as far as famous Alpine Passes were concerned, more comprehensive. Newly developed small cars with tiny engines were making tremendous progress in those postwar years. This caused havoc in the handicap system of staggered prescribed average speeds between small and large cubic capacity classes. Thus, in 1950, out of the seven Coupes des Alpes awarded, no less than six went to the 610cc Dyna-Panhards (750 class won by Edmond Signoret/Elie Guibourdenche). Before these results became final, there were heated discussions about the size of their inlet manifolds. At first two of these Panhards were stricken from the results list, finally to be reinstated. The seventh Coupe des Alpes went to Ian Appleyard in the new XK 120 Jaguar registered NUB 120. He put up fastest time of the day both in the Col du Var hill climb and in the 'flying kilometre' on the Italian Autostrada. His co-pilot this time was William Lyons's daughter Patricia, whom Ian Appleyard had married two months before the Alpine. Amongst the rallying fraternity, winning a Coupe des Alpes was considered the ultimate achievement. With Norman Garrad now in charge of the works Sunbeam-Talbots, all three team cars (Murray-Frame, George Hartwell and Garrad) were classified, George Murray-Frame/John Pearman winning the

Pordoi and Falzarego Passes, the previous year's Cup winner Gautruche in his Citroën 11 légère (certainly not the most powerful car!). Next came the timed Stelvio Hill Climb which saw Leonard Potter (Allard) as the winner, followed by Donald

two litre class. The team award went to Panhard (Signoret, Masset and Guy Lapchin), the one for non-French makes to MG (Kenk, JH Keller and Ernest de Regibus). The Swiss equipe Kenk/Harry Zweifel also won the 1500 class. One must not fail to mention that Agostino di Stefano/Ercole in an Alfa Romeo 2500 6C won the three litre class, the first ever Alfa Romeo class win in the French Alpine.

The organizing team of the Coupe des Alpes with René Carrière as Clerk of the Course, formerly a driver of high repute, was quick to adjust its engine size handicaps for 1951, with due consideration for technical progress. Fairness was thereby re-established without delay, whilst some other rallies continued with outdated handicaps for quite a number of years. Of the ten Coupes des Alpes awarded in 1951, no less than seven went to British makes. In the unlimited class there were two Jaguar XK 120s (class winner Ian Appleyard and Swiss Rolf Habisreutinger) and a Cadillac-Allard (Godfrey 'Goff' Imhoff). Tommy Wisdom (Aston Martin) and Edgar Wadsworth (Healey) tied for the three litre class win, both gaining a coveted Alpine Cup. A Bristol/BMW engined Frazer Nash (George Duff/Eric Winterbottom) won a Cup and the two litre class (from Roberto Piodi, also a Cup winner, in a Lancia Aurelia B20). HRG, so prominent in more than one post-war French Alpine, scored its last major success; John Gott winning a Coupe des Alpes and the 1500 class, with Bill Shepherd taking second place in a similar car. This left only the 1100 and 750 classes and one Coupe des Alpes each to the French contingent: Dr Marc & Mme Angelvin in a Simca 8 and M & Mme François Landon in a Renault 4CV. The Team Prize went to Jaguar, with Appleyard, Habisreutinger, and Spaniard Soler.

Those were the heydays of the French Alpine. Without a shadow of doubt it was considered the toughest, fairest, and best-organized rally of them all. It surpassed the Monte Carlo Rally certainly in quality of the participants, if not in quantity. Under the chairmanship of Baron d'Huart the three former top drivers Carrière, Avril and Descollas worked effectively together as Stewards. The prestige of the AC de Marseille et Provence was high. The ability of this Club in the South of France to integrate the Dolomites and South Tyrol into the rally as its very centrepiece certainly was a major success factor.

This became possible because Northern Italy was as quick as France to welcome motor sport back after World

Godfrey 'Goff' Imhof and his Cadillac-Allard brought home a 1951 Alpine Cup. The picture shows him and co-driver Tom Lush in the 1952 event when he was not so successful.

War II. In 1947 the regional Italian Automobile Club di Trento under its newly elected president Count Sigismondo Manci introduced a new cross-breed between rally and road race called the Stella Alpina, or Edelweiss. Start and finish was in Trento, and there were four daily stages or loops including all the famous Dolomite passes. Over the years the total distance varied between 700 and 900 miles. From its beginning the Stella Alpina attracted many drivers of repute, like Piero Taruffi who won the first edition of the Stella with his Lancia Aprilia touring car. By 1948 an armaments race had begun, and Taruffi was back with a Cisitalia sports car. His main opponent was Nuccio Bertone, the famous stylist, who drove a very racy Fiat Stanguellini 1100 S sports car. The battle was still undecided when Taruffi was forced to retire at the Stelvio, the Cisitalia being plagued with technical problems. That gave victory to Bertone and his Stanguellini. In 1949 Francesco Simontacchi

For nine years the Automobile Club of Trento organized its very sporting Stella Alpina (Edelweiss) Rally, which in 1955 (when the French Alpine was cancelled due to the Le Mans disaster) attracted all the prominent Alpine specialists. It was won by Olivier Gendebien/Mlle Gilberte Thirion (the latter at the wheel) in a Mercedes 300 SL.

Crespi (Alfa Romeo 1900 SS) were victorious in 1952 and 1954 respectively. Till now, Italian drivers always dominated the Stella Alpina, but the last one – of 1955 – was to go to the all-Belgian equipe Olivier Gendebien/Mlle Gilberte Thirion in a Mercedes 300 SL. Another 300 SL driven by Spaniard Salvador Fabregas Bas was second and Ferdinando Gatta (Lancia Aurelia B20 GT 2500), Gianni Lancia's brother-in-law third. Tourist traffic and safety problems then sadly brought the Stella Alpina to an end, very much like the Mille Miglia and the Coppa d'Oro delle Dolomiti.

Back now to the Rallye International des Alpes. For 1952 a General Classification was formally introduced, thus leading many other major European rallies into a new and more modern phase of motor sport. Starting in Marseille, the 95 cars soon passed into Italy, with the Dolomite circuit round Cortina as a centrepiece. From there the route led into Austria, briefly back into Italy to cover the Stelvio, with a short spell in Switzerland, then returning to France via Italy, to the finish in Cannes. Seven years after VE Day the early post war era appeared to be over, but this was not, in fact, the case. There still was one pre-war model in the rally which was good for a big surprise. Lo and behold, Alex von Falkenhausen in the BMW 328 was second fastest to Ian Appleyard's Jaguar in the timed section covering the Pordoi and Falzarego Passes into Cortina. Then he put up a fastest time of the day at the Stelvio ahead of Appleyard, and was second behind Maurice Gatsonides (Jaguar XK 120) at the Col d'Izoard. Only 23 cars made it to the finish at Cannes, and ten of these received Alpine Cups for an unpenalized run. Thus the performance in the timed Hill Climbs was decisive for the first ten places in general classification. This established von Falkenhausen as the outright winner, from Dutchman Maurice Gatsonides, Frenchman Ernest de Regibus (Renault 4CV), and Ian Appleyard in his Jaguar. The latter, it must be said in all fairness, was more interested in winning the first ever Gold Cup of the the French Alpine which he duly did for his three consecutive Coupes des Alpes in 1950, 1951 and 1952. He nursed the legendary NUB 120 over the tricky sections, rather than go for an outright win and risk the Coupe d'Or.

Falkenhausen was one of the leading technicians with BMW to whom HJ Aldington offered a job in England just after the war. While his colleague Fritz Fiedler accepted,

repeated the Stanguellini success, and Count Johnny Lurani was fifth driving one of the rare Bristol 400s. Maria Teresa de Filippis, who later tried her luck in Formula 1 with a 250 Maserati, was at the wheel of a small Urania sports car fitted with a flat twin BMW 750 motorcycle engine with which she managed sixth place overall.

Then came local hero Salvatore Ammendola who scored outright wins in 1950 (Alfa Romeo 2500), 1951 (Ferrari 195 Inter Coupé) and 1953. In September 1953 he led the onslaught of three Lancia Aurelia B20 GT 2500s, winning ahead of Enrico Anselmi and Piero Valenzano. By now the Stella Alpina was rivalling the Coppa d'Oro delle Dolomiti, the road race over the Dolomite circuit also used in the French Alpine Rally. Ovidio Capelli (Fiat V8 Zagato) and Giuseppe

Baron Alex von Falkenhausen, accompanied by his wife Kitty (sister of Count Heinrich von der Mühle), was the outright winner of the 1952 French Alpine, a remarkable achievement with his pre-war BMW 328.

Falkenhausen decided to set up his own company in Munich, AFM, which stood for 'Alex Falkenhausen Munich'. Building BMW-engined Formula 2 racing cars, he survived the hard way until BMW became operational again. During these early post war years, Falkenhausen also did some rallying in a superbly prepared pre-war BMW 328 which he also took to the 1952 French Alpine. A Dyna-Panhard (René Fabre) and another 4CV Renault (Picon) took places 5 and 6, perhaps slightly favoured by the handicap. Then came the last four Coupe des Alpes winners, a Lancia Aurelia GT (Ferdinando Gatta, with

Falkenhausen's success was perhaps made a bit easier as Ian Appleyard in his XK 120 drove very cautiously so as not to endanger the first ever Alpine Gold Cup offered for three Coupes des Alpes wins in a row. In this the Scotsman succeeded brilliantly.

47

1953 saw Porsche triumphant, with six Coupes des Alpes
for the type 356 1500 model, and an outright win by Helmut
Polensky (centre)/Walter Schlüter seen here with Mlle Gilberte
Thirion protecting her coiffure against wind and weather.
Polensky/Schlüter went on to win the first ever European Rally
Championship that year.

Another Coupe des Alpes for the Falkenhausen couple, this
time (1953) driving a Frazer Nash on loan from their old friend
HJ Aldington.

Belgian journalist Jacques Ickx as co-driver) and the three
Sunbeam Talbot 90s of Murray-Frame, Mike Hawthorn, and
Stirling Moss, an interesting mix of top rallymen and promising
Grand Prix drivers. The Sunbeams, now fitted with the new 2.3
litre engine, won the Team Prize, and Murray-Frame was the
winner of the three litre class. Max Nathan, of Germany, was
11th overall in his 1500 Porsche, the only class winner without
a Coupe des Alpes. Altogether, 23 cars survived, including
five driven by Britons, Tommy Wisdom (Aston-Martin) being
amongst these in 15th position.

1953 witnessed the advent of the European Rally
Championship, then called the Championnat d'Europe de
Grand Tourisme. Also, there were new cylinder capacity
classes: up to 750, 1000, 1300, 1600, 2000, 2600, and
unlimited. This time, the route provided for the inclusion of
Germany, so the itinerary now passed through the same five
countries traditionally traversed by the International Alpine
Trials between the wars. Another novelty was the inclusion of
the notoriously dangerous Gavia Pass which, together with the
Vivione, was to become the most fearful section of the French
Alpine in years to come. 102 cars started in Marseille, and

Ian and Pat Appleyard in their new steel-bodied XK 120 won their fifth Coupe des Alpes in 1953, a record equalled only by René Trautmann in 1968.

54 of them arrived back at the finish in Cannes. An unusually large number of 25 made it with a clean sheet and, therefore, could claim Alpine Cups. This was an all-time high never to be repeated, and an indication that the 1953 edition was a bit easier than any other.

Impressive was the dominating rôle of Porsche, winning six Coupes des Alpes and taking first, second, and fourth place in general classification, as well as the Team Prize (Helmut Polensky, Rudi Sauerwein, and Kurt Zeller). The order was Polensky (partnered by Walter, Schlüter on their way to become the first ever European Rally Champions), Sauerwein, then the Belgian Ferrari two litre of Jacques Herzet ahead of Kurt Zeller. Ian Appleyard was fifth in his new and slightly heavier steel-bodied Jaguar XK 120 (registered RUB 120) but this did not keep him from recording the fastest time of the day at the Stelvio and the Izoard (Habisreutinger in a similar

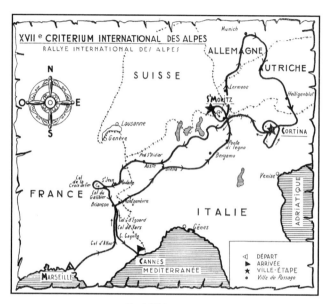

The 1954 itinerary.

Fifteen years after winning a Coupe des Alpes in a BMW 328 (1939), Austrian Wolfgang Denzel was back to score another outright win in his Volkswagen-based Denzel 1300 sports car, which he built in small numbers in Vienna. He is accompanied here by his chief engineer Hubert Stroinigg.

car was fastest at the Pordoi and the Petit Saint Bernard but dropped out on the last leg due to an accident). Sixth – and only marginally behind Appleyard on bonus points – was Alex von Falkenhausen, this time in a Frazer Nash with BMW-based engine.

The Rootes Group competed with six of its new Sunbeam Alpine two seater models, originally conceived by a Sunbeam dealer in Bournemouth named George Hartwell. On his own initiative he had converted a Sunbeam Talbot 90 drophead into a very chic roadster, an idea quickly taken up by the works. It was a sturdy sporting model, but with its virtually unchanged 2.3 litre engine its power-to-weight ratio was unexciting, to say the least. Four of the works cars, driven by Stirling Moss, Murray-Frame, the American John Fitch, and Miss Sheila van Damm, won Alpine Cups. The latter was also awarded the Coupe des Dames. The daughter of Vivian van Damm, Manager of the Windmill Theatre, with the wartime slogan of 'We Never Closed', brought a lot of publicity but had also become a highly competent rally driver. Jaguar (Ian and Pat

Baroness d'Huart Saint Mauris, wife of the Automobile Club de Marseille et Provence's president, congratulates Wolfgang Denzel.

In between a full Formula 1 season in his 250F Maserati, Stirling Moss brought the Sunbeam Alpine home with a clean sheet, to win a Coupe des Alpes the way he had done in 1952 and 1953.

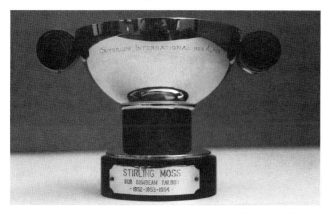

Moss was awarded the second and penultimate Alpine Gold Cup.

Appleyard, Olivier Gendebien/Charles Fraikin, as well as Reg and Joan Mansbridge) Lancia (Ferdinando Gatta, Count Johnny Lurani, and Salvador Fabregas-Bas) and Panhard (Raymond Stempert, Marcel Schwob d'Héricourt, and Chieusse) scored three Alpine Cups each.

Two new sports car models from major British manufacturers made their bow in the 1954 Alpine, Austin-

Healey and Triumph, to compete with the Jaguars and Sunbeam Alpines. The French industry, with its emphasis on small capacity bread-and butter saloons, was essentially represented by highly tuned and surprisingly fast special versions of the Renault 4CV and Peugeot 203.

Following the previous year's Porsche walkover, the required speeds for the 1600cc class were stiffened considerably for 1954.

Apart from reducing Switzerland's rôle to the provision of an overnight stop at St Moritz, the itinerary followed traditional lines. But then came miserable weather with lots of snow (in mid-July). This taxed the Automobile Club de Marseille et Provence to the limit but despite the need for considerable last-minute route changes, the organization passed this severe test with flying colours. Grossglockner and Gavia were completely blocked. Both the Stelvio and the Izoard which featured more than once in the itinerary, both had to be circumvented on at least one occasion. The 79 starters were up for a hard time. The first special test was held during a downpour on the Munich to Salzburg Autobahn over 1½ kilometres with a flying start. Here Ian Appleyard's RUB 120 scored fastest time, driven by its new owner Dennis Scott. The O'Hara Moore/John Gott Frazer-Nash was second fastest, but Wolfgang Denzel in his rear-engined VW-based 1300cc Denzel built in Vienna was only one tenth of a second slower, third fastest of the day. Of the seven Sunbeam Alpines entered, only Stirling Moss managed to pass this test without penalty, by the tiny margin of 0.2 seconds. All the other Sunbeams buried their dreams of Alpine Cups on this stretch of Autobahn. On the third day cars took off from Cortina d'Ampezzo for the Dolomite Circuit, with its timed section over the Pordoi and the Falzarego Passes. This was also won by Scott in the Jaguar, but remarkably Denzel was second fastest overall, leaving Bill Burton in an Aston Martin, Georges Houel (Alfa Romeo 1900) and all the others well behind him. Denzel consistently proved to be the only small capacity car in the field able to stand up to the 'big boys', even on a scratch basis. In the next timed test, the Stelvio, DG Scott's Jaguar was again fastest of them all, followed by the Henry O'Hara Moore Frazer-Nash, the Bill Burton Aston Martin – and the little Denzel! Landslides had made the Izoard impassable, so the Col de la Cayolle was hastily selected as the last of the timed hill climbs. As the Scott Jaguar with a broken rear spring

A new British sports car, the Triumph TR2, had its first go at the Alpine in 1954, Dutchman Maurice Gatsonides winning an Alpine Cup. Shown here are ACL Mills/Done at the starting ramp in Marseilles.

The new Alfa Romeo Giulietta Sprint of Michel Collange/Robert Huguet scored an outright win in the 1956 rally, leaving behind two Porsche Carreras in the general classification.

was no longer in perfect condition, it was Eric Haddon's turn in another XK 120 to put up fastest time of day. Wolfgang Denzel, however, stayed in striking distance and left Aston-Martin, Frazer-Nash, as well as the fast and sturdy Triumph TR2s of Maurice Gatsonides and others, behind.

Finally, 37 cars arrived in Cannes, 11 of them with clean sheets to claim a Coupe des Alpes. Bonus points for the performance in the timed tests, therefore, decided the sequence in general classification. The outright winner by a vast margin was Wolfgang Denzel with his co-driver and chief engineer Hubert Stroinigg. The little Denzel's times would have stood many a three litre car in good stead. Second and third were the two highly tuned Renault 4CVs driven by Jean Rédélé/ Louis Pons and Yves Lesur/Maurice Foulgoc. Rédélé, a young Renault dealer and 4CV-tuner in Dieppe, was immensely proud of his Coupe des Alpes. Soon after his great achievement he built a Renault-based sports coupé which he baptized 'Alpine'. It was the beginning of a new make with a great rallying future.

Fourth overall and two litre class winners were LtCol Henry O'Hara Moore/John Gott (Frazer Nash) followed by Paul Guiraud/Henri Beau (Peugeot 203) and Maurice Gatsonides/ Rob Slotemaker in the new Triumph TR2 at its first Alpine outing. An Aston Martin (Bill Burton/Burke) was seventh, the best Standard Touring Car (Heinz Meier/Hermann Luba, DKW) eighth. The last three of the eleven Alpine Cup winners were Roger Rauch/Bousson (Salmson 2300S), Stirling Moss/John Cutts (Sunbeam Alpine), and Paul Barbier/Rastit (Peugeot 203). Clearly, the Sunbeam Alpine had reached the end of its development, although sturdy and reliable it was no longer up to its rivals in performance. Moss, despite all his artistry in driving, managed only third place in the 2600cc class but he was followed home by four more Sunbeams (Murray-Frame, Sheila van Damm, Orr and Hartwell). It is all the more remarkable that he won a Gold Cup for his three Coupes des Alpes in a row (1952, 1953 and 1954). This award must be rated even higher than Ian Appleyard's two years earlier. The Scotsman's Jaguar XK 120 was always the most powerful car in the field which cannot be said about the underpowered 2.3 litre Sunbeams.

A separate classification for the European Rally Championship (open to Standard Touring Cars only) was also drawn up. It was headed by Alpine Cup winners Heinz Meier/Hermann Luba (DKW), with penalty laden Kurt Zeller (Fiat 1100) and Walter Schlüter (DKW) in second and third positions. The latter was proclaimed European Champion by the end of the year. The Team Prize went to Triumph with the TR2 (Gatsonides, Hans Kat/Joseph Tak and Ken Richardson), whilst Sheila van Damm/Anne Hall won the Ladies Cup once again. Class winners without Alpine Cups were Yves Barre (Porsche, 1600cc) and Eric Haddon (Jaguar, unlimited).

The 1955 event was cancelled following the Le Mans disaster, but for 1956 the Critérium International des Alpes was back to normal. There were substantial alterations in the itinerary. Germany, Austria and Switzerland (almost) were left out, for the benefit of Yugoslavia. Traffic problems with increased tourist travel in the month of July was the main reason for this change. The East offered sufficiently wild and totally uncongested routes as an alternative. Amongst the special tests, there was one lap of the Monza Road Circuit. Beyond the Dolomites, on the way to Zagreb, fairly easy transport stages made life more comfortable for competitors. At Zagreb a speed test over a distance of 1.5 kilometres with a flying start was held to provide a spectacle for the Croatian public. Before leaving Yugoslavia the itinerary led over the rough and majestic Vršič Pass (called Moistrocca when part of Italy during the inter-war years), tough and unknown to most participants. The timed hill climbs were held at the Falzarego, the Stelvio, and the Col d'Izoard.

New models were coming to the fore. In the 1600 class five of the new MGAs were competing with the Rootes Group's five new Sunbeam Rapiers (replacing the old Sunbeam Alpine)

and the far more powerful Porsche Carrera models. The 2 litre class was swamped with works Triumphs in improved TR3 form. In the 1300 class were three Austrian Denzels, one of them driven by Edgar Wadsworth, in former years seen at the wheel of a Silverstone Healey. They did not have it all their own way, though, since Alfa Romeo had brought out the light and fast Giulietta Sprint, with 80 to 90bhp in standard form.

For the first time in international rallying the small Alfa Romeo Giulietta Sprint achieved an outright win, ably driven by Michel Collange/Robert Huguet, and leaving behind two Porsche Carreras (Claude Storez/Robert Buchet and Americans Chuck Wayne/DD Kriplen) as well as the Denzel of André Blanchard/Guy Jouanneaux (with yet another Denzel, brothers Marcel & F Lauga in 9th place). The first 'big banger' was a Ferrari 250 GT driven by Jean-Pierre Estager/Jean Pebrel, in fifth place. Out of 83 starters there were 34 survivors, 17 of them with a clean sheet and, consequently, a Coupe des Alpes. No fewer than five Triumph TR3s won Alpine Cups, and the Team Prize as well. All in all, British cars collected 9, German cars 3, Austrian and Italian cars 2 Coupes des Alpes each, and there was a single one for P David's Peugeot 203. Other class winners, apart from Collange, Storez and Estager, were Maurice Gatsonides/Ed Pennybacker (Triumph TR3, 2000cc class, 8th overall), Cuth and Edward Harrison (Ford Zephyr, 2600cc class, 7th), and Dr Barker/Don Cooke (Standard Ten, 1000cc class, 32nd overall, the only class winner without an Alpine Cup). The Coupe des Dames went to Mrs Nancy Mitchell/Miss Pat Faichney (MGA, 15th overall, also winning a Coupe des Alpes).

Major floods and the Suez Crisis contributed to the cancellation of the 1957 French Alpine. In those days the AC de Marseilles et Provence was also struck by major internal upheavals. A number of excellent officials had given up their positions. Times were changing, and new forces were pushing to get into the 'Association Sportive'. This was not at all to the liking of Baron d'Huart, a strong-willed and somewhat authoritarian gentleman. For twenty years he had presided over the Club and led it to the greatest possible international esteem. Now he had had enough of it. His successor was Amédée Marquis de Bretteville a charming gentleman, tall and blond, and very conciliatory. In the Club Committee there always had been very diverging opinions as to how the rally

Robert Buchet/Claude Storez drove their Porsche Carrera into second place behind the Giulietta Sprint.

should be developed, and how tough it should be. Strategically these debates now led to a zig-zag course very detrimental to the wellbeing of the Critérium International des Alpes.

For 1958, the itinerary was greatly changed, the Dolomite Circuit, Austria, Yugoslavia and Germany were no longer included. The number of starters was down to 58. The French contingent was tiny in numbers and the rally only existed

thanks to strong British support. Based on his experience in all the events since 1947, the British motoring writer Joe Lowrey described the French Alpine as going through a bad patch. The organization was no longer quite up to its old standards, possibly in part attributable to a very serious accident of Jean-Marie Catalin, the Secretary General and Clerk of the Course, during the rally. Given prevailing conditions the prescribed time

André Baron d'Huart Saint Mauris congratulates Nancy Mitchell who, with her new MGA, won both a Coupe des Alpes and the Ladies' Prize in the 1956 rally. For 20 years the Baron had presided over the Automobile Club de Marseilles et Provence. During these years the French Alpine developed from small beginnings to become the best run and toughest rally of them all.

for some of the special tests were impossible to achieve. Had the organizers stuck to the regulations rigorously, no Coupe des Alpes would have been awarded at all. However, there were valid reasons for clemency over the Mont Revard, Izoard, and

Soubeyrand sections, and thus seven Coupes des Alpes were attributed. Alfa Romeo celebrated a triple victory with a variety of Giulietta models. Bernard Consten/Roger de Lageneste were the outright winners in a Zagato Sprint Veloce model, with Guy Clarou/Pierre Gelé second and Max Riess/Hans Wencher third in touring Giuliettas. The remaining four Alpine Cups went to British makes, the Triumph of Keith Ballisat/Alain Bertaut being fourth, and winning the over 1600 unlimited class. In fifth place, the Ford Zephyr of Edward Harrison/BPR Haberson was best standard touring car over 1600cc, just ahead of Peter Harper/Peter Jopp (Sunbeam Rapier), winners of the 1600cc class. The seventh Cup went to Bill Shepherd/John Williamson in a big Austin-Healey 100. With a total delay of 5 minutes, Pat Moss/Ann Wisdom drove into Marseilles in 10th position overall, to win the Coupe des Dames. John Sprinzel/Willy Cave (Austin-Healey Sprite) won the 1000cc class, and was 15th overall out of the 25 that arrived at the finish.

The 1959 Criterium International des Alpes presented itself in a new light. The regulations were drastically changed and the imposed handicaps favoured Touring Cars over GT Cars, and small cars over big ones. This attracted Renault with a powerful team of very fast Dauphine models but otherwise the entries stagnated. There were 59 starters, one up from last year. This time the itinerary included some of the toughest sections of the Austrian Alpine Rally, including the notorious Turracher Höhe with its gradient of 1 in 3. That very rough and rutted route had been included in the 1934 International Alpine Trial. In those days the Singer cars could only climb the hill in reverse gear. This unorthodox mode persisted well into the mid-fifties in the Austrian Alpine Rally, practiced by such makes as Aero Minor, Gutbrod, and Lloyd.

From the start at the Quai of the Old Port of Marseilles, the first speed hill climb was soon reached. Col d'Allos was an easy prey to Robert Buchet in a type 550 Porsche Spyder, but three Renault Dauphines (Jacques Feret/Guy Monraisse, Guy Clarou, and Paul Condriller) took the lead on handicap, having accumulated masses of bonus points while the larger Grand Tourers had to go full steam ahead not to be penalized. The speed test on the Monza Circuit produced similar results. Walter Schock/Tak in their Mercedes 300 SL were fastest overall, but the three Dauphines now led from Olympic skiing ace Henri Oreiller in his Alfa Giulietta TI Touring Car (1300cc).

Bernard Consten/Roger de Lageneste drove their Alfa Giulietta
Sprint Zagato to victory in the 1958 French Alpine now called
Coupe des Alpes.

Rules for the 1959 Coupe des Alpes favoured
small cars over big ones, and touring cars
over GT cars. Paul Condriller/Georges Robin
were the outright winners in their very fast
works Renault Dauphine.

The drop-out rate of GT cars was high, while smaller Touring
Cars had no difficulty in meeting their schedule.

A good example was the tight Greifenburg section as cars
streamed into Austria, with Kreuzberg and Turrach still to
follow. Via Innsbruck back into Italy, Oreiller's Alfa was fastest
up the timed Vivione, with a Dauphine, remarkably, in second
place on scratch! The GTs had shot their bolt! So everything
looked like a Renault hat-trick, with the Oreiller/Fernand
Masoero Alfa Giulietta likely to take fourth place.

Then, back in France and travelling in a southerly direction,
bad fortune struck. First, the Giulietta gearbox seized, then
Mont Ventoux turned into a Renault Waterloo. Monraisse
collected penalties for clocking in too early, and Clarou was
out with clutch failure. Of the 27 survivors, eight Touring Cars
and one GT were free of penalties, and good for a Coupe des
Alpes. Not unexpectedly, the overall order was Paul Condriller/

Pat Moss/Ann Wisdom drove their Austin-Healey 3000 into second place overall in 1960. Stirling's sister and the daughter of Tommy Wisdom thus recorded the best ever ladies result.

Only the Austin-Healey 3000 of Donald and Erle Morley arrived at the 1961 finish without loss of marks, a performance reminiscent of Gaston Gautruche in 1949. The twin brothers, however, went one better and added another overall win in 1962 to their laurels.

Georges Robin (Renault Dauphine), Hermann Kühne/Hans Wencher (DKW Auto-Union), Paddy Hopkirk/Jack Scott (Sunbeam Rapier) and Jacques Rey/André Guilhaudin (DB-Panhard), the only GT car of the lot. Then, in fifth place came

the Ford Zephyr of Peter Riley/Alex Pitts as the best car over two litres. The remaining Alpine Cup winners were Peter Jopp/ Les Leston (Sunbeam Rapier, 6th), Cuth & John Harrison (Ford Zephyr, 7th), Edward Harrison/Fleetwood (Ford Zephyr, 8th) and ID 'Tiny' Lewis/Tony Nash (Triumph Herald, 9th). The Team Prize, understandably, went to Ford after a remarkable show of speed and stamina.

In 1960 the rally was a somewhat abridged version of 1870 miles, and without the famous Dolomite Circuit which, since 1958, was no longer available. However, the previous year's handicap mistake had been put right, and a good balance between touring and GT cars of all sizes was struck. The programme was condensed into two stages, and 65 starters took off from Marseilles to head for the night rest at Chamonix via the dreaded Gavia and Vivione Passes, which meant many miles of the easy North Italian plains. The route was spiced with a number of special tests, however, beginning with La Couronne, where Oreiller/Masoero were fastest in their Giulietta SS Zagato, ahead of Pat Moss/Ann Riley (née Wisdom) in the Austin-Healey 3000. Mont Ventoux saw two Giulietta Zagatos (Oreiller and Roger de Lageneste/Henri Greder) in front, followed by the Ferrari of Gérard Spinedi/ Briffaut. The Jaguar of O'Connor did the fastest Monza lap (and soon afterwards retired), with Pat Moss second and Oreiller tying with Don and Erle Morley (Austin-Healey) for third position. At Chamonix the interim order was first Oreiller, second Pat Moss, and third José Behra/R Richard in a 3.8 litre Jaguar saloon. The shorter return leg to Cannes with five special stages proved far more difficult and reduced the field to 39 arrivals. At the Izoard the two Alfas were again fastest, followed by Buchet in a Porsche and the Austin-Healeys of Pat Moss and the Morley brothers. Oreiller looked the likely winner, when a puncture in the last special stage caused him a delay of almost half a minute, dropping him to seventh place overall, just behind the glorious six who received Alpine Cups: Roger de Lageneste (Alfa Giulietta SS Zagato) thus became the outright winner followed home by Pat Moss (Austin-Healey 3000), also winning the Coupe des Dames. Third place went to the best Touring Car, the 3.8 litre Jaguar of José Behra, the brother of the late lamented Jeannot of Formula 1 fame, followed by three more Tourers, Eugen Böhringer/Hermann Socher (Mercedes 220 SE), G Parkes/G Howarth (Jaguar 3.8), and René Trautmann/Claude Ogier (Citroen ID 19). The Team Prize went to the Austin-Healey 3000 of Pat Moss, John Gott/William Shepherd (8th overall) and D & E Morley (14th overall). 9th in general classification and 1600 Touring Car class winners were Peter Harper/Peter Procter (Sunbeam Rapier). Altogether, British cars scored five class wins, French cars two (Citroën, Trautmann, and Renault Dauphine, Nicholas/Devaux), while the 1600 GT class went to Robert Buchet's German Porsche, and the 1300 GT class, of course, to Alfa Romeo, from Italy.

With so many of the classic mountain passes no longer available for rallying the organizers were searching for a new format. They established the principle to distinguish between the necessary evil of easy 'liason sections' with a standard 50kph average for transport purposes, selective sections with a more demanding time schedule, and timed épreuves. For 1961 a total of 25 selective sections and 7 épreuves were imposed on the 1857 mile itinerary through France, Italy and a short stretch in Switzerland. 66 cars took off from Marseilles, soon to attack timed hill climbs at St Baume and Mont Ventoux. In both of these épreuves the Hans Joachim Walter/Hans Wencher Porsche Super 90 put up the fastest time of the day. Both of the two Alfa Romeo stars retired on the majestic Mont Ventoux, Henri Oreiller running out of road and Roger de Lageneste with engine trouble. Tight schedules as well as navigation problems reduced the field to 34 cars by the time the overnight stop at Chamonix was reached. Only three cars arrived there with a clean sheet, and Hans Joachim Walter now led from the two Austin-Healey 3000s of the Morley twins and Peter Riley/Tony Ambrose. Then came the Gran San Bernardo Hill Climb where Walter retired his Porsche with engine trouble, and the Monza speed test which saw the Mercedes 300 SL of Eugen Böhringer/Hermann Socher fastest of them all. The Vivione was more atrocious than ever, the fiendish Gavia had to be cut out of the route once again, and on to the Stelvio Hill Climb where Peter Riley was out after a crash, and the Morleys were fastest, ahead of Böhringer's 300 SL. This left Don and Erle Morley in the Austin-Healey as the only ones with a clean sheet, and merely the Izoard and Col d'Allos épreuves still to tackle. It was in this latter climb that Jean Rolland (Alfa Giulietta Zagato) showed his mettle by scoring fastest time. He lived in Digne, in the Alpes de Provence, and was soon to become 'the favourite son' for the local fans. In Cannes the Morleys were celebrated

as heroes for theirs was the only Coupe des Alpes, and the outright win in the rally. Second place went to Rolland/Gabriel Augias, ahead of Paddy Hopkirk/Jack Scott (Sunbeam Rapier), Henri Greder/J Charron (Renault Alpine), Peter Harper/Peter Procter (Sunbeam Rapier), René Trautmann/Jean-Claude Ogier (Citroën ID 19), and Keith Ballisat/ID Lewis (Sunbeam Rapier). Very deservedly the Team Prize went to the three Sunbeam Rapiers listed above, and Ewy Rosqvist/Monika Wallraff in their Volvo won the Coupe des Dames.

In its strategy for developing the Critérium International des Alpes, the AC de Marseille et Provence steered a zig-zag course which resulted in drastically diminishing entries. In 1962 only 48 cars were sent on their way from Marseille on a tour of over 2400 miles, first to an overnight stop at Brescia, then on a combined Dolomite-cum-Apennine circuit reminiscent of the Mille Miglia, and finally the third stage from Brescia to Cannes.

The rather unfortunate animator of the last three events, Henri Oreiller, switched from Alfa Romeo to a Ferrari. With his new mount he was fastest in four of the first timed tests (St Baume, Mont Ventoux, Col de Rousset, and Monza) as well as second at the St Jean-en-Royans circuit to the Morley brothers' Austin-Healey. At Brescia, therefore, he was leading comfortably, and there were only 7 retirements up to this first night stop. However, the Oreiller/Burglin Ferrari broke a half-shaft on the Rolle Pass, and from then on the outright win was to be disputed between the Austin-Healeys and 1961 European Rally Champion Hans Joachim Walter in his Porsche. 12 cars were back in Brescia with clean sheets, to commence the return stage to Cannes. The Stelvio was blocked by snow and, consequently, deleted from the itinerary, but the dreaded Vivione caused a reduction to only five cars with clean sheets. 28 cars arrived at Cannes, and five of them were awarded Coupes des Alpes. The order in General Classification, therefore, was Don and Erle Morley (Austin-Healey 3000), Hans Joachim Walter/Kurt Schoettler (Porsche Carrera), Pat Moss/Pauline Mayman (Austin-Healey), Mike Sutcliffe/Roy Fidler (Triumph TR4), and René Trautmann/Patrick Chopin (Citroën DS 19), the only Touring Car without penalty.

Austin-Healey swept the board, not only with another outright Morley victory, but also with the Coupe des Dames and the Manufacturers' Team Prize (Morley, Moss and David Seigle-Morris/Tony Ambrose, 8th overall).

Jean Rolland lived at Digne in the Alpes de Provence and quickly became the local hero, with three outright wins to his credit, in 1963 (picture, Alfa Giulietta Zagato), 1964 and 1966, an unrivalled achievement. Ably supported by Roland Augias, a mathematics professor, Rolland won all three Coupes driving Alfa Romeos.

With only 48 starters, the Criterium des Alpes had reached its nadir in 1962. It was time for a change, and luckily the right man was called in to give the rally a new sense of direction. His name was Victor Joullie-Duclos, and he had more than a decade of organisational experience with the event in subordinate positions. He realized that the present road traffic situation made nonsense of the old dream to unite all the major Alpine Passes and thoroughfares in five or six countries under one single umbrella. His logical concept meant a concentration within the French Alps, with a minor excursion into nearby Italy and Switzerland, for transnational window dressing. The way the 1963 regulations were presented to industry and leading drivers went a long way to restore confidence. The number of starters increased to 78. A tremendous array of fast GT cars, like the Austin-Healey 3000 and Triumph TR4 works cars, were confronted with strong contingents of Touring Cars including 16 Mini Coopers, about a dozen Renaults, numerous Citroën ID/DS 19s, Ford Cortinas, Mercedes 220 SEs and Sunbeam Rapiers. The 2356 mile itinerary was divided in three major sections, with night stops at Briançon and Chamonix. The first three speed hill climbs of Section 1 were won by Paddy Hopkirk (Austin-Healey, St Baume), Robert Buchet (Abarth-Porsche, Mont Ventoux), and Timo Mäkinen (Austin-Healey, Cayolle). Of the 26 retirements up to Briançon there was an unusually high proportion of fast GT cars, including Hopkirk. At the Rousset Hill Climb Buchet in the Abarth-Porsche was again the winner, and the Morley twins (Austin-Healey) were fastest on the St Jean-en-Royans circuit, as well as the Col du Luittel. The Rauno Aaltonen/Tony Ambrose Morris Mini Cooper S 1275 was tremendously fast, taking the lead amongst the Touring Cars, with Henri Greder in the big 4.2 litre Ford Falcon V8 in second place until his retirement. By the time Chamonix was reached all the Triumph TR4s were out, and so was Buchet, in the Abarth-Porsche, whose engine had blown up. Only seven cars still showed clean sheets, amongst them just two GT cars, the Morleys and the Giulietta Zagato of Jean Rolland/Gabriel Augias. So on the Switzerland and over the Gran San Bernardo into Italy, heading for Monza where the

Having won three Alpine Cups for Citroën, René Trautmann switched to Lancia for an outright win in the 1965 Alpine, accompanied by Claudine Bouchet, soon to become Mrs Trautmann.

France takes over 1938-1971

On his way to the 1966 European Rally Championship Günter Klass won the GT category in that year's French Alpine, driving a Porsche 911. His co-driver, Rolf Wütherich, had been James Dean's mechanic, surviving the film star's crash in a Porsche Spyder.

Morleys were again fastest of them all. They were well on their way to a Coupe d'Or for three consecutive Alpine Cups. But it was not to be: During the last night the Austin-Healey's final drive gear went solid, and the last of the Austin-Healeys was out! Rolland could afford to nurse his Alfa in the last two hill climbs, both held at the Col d'Allos, the first one going to Henry Taylor (Ford Cortina), the second to Aaltonen's Mini. Thus the outright win went to Jean Rolland, followed by the five Touring Cars of Aaltonen, Henry Taylor/Brian Melia, David Seigle-Morris/Hercock (both Ford Cortina GT), René Trautmann/Cherel (Citroën DS 19), and Pauline Mayman/Valerie Domleo (Morris Mini Cooper 997cc). Despite the Austin-Healey disaster the British Motor Corporation had reason to celebrate. Its Minis won two Alpine Cups, the Team Prize, and the Coupe des Dames: Pauline Mayman, formerly co-pilot to Pat Moss, had progressed to full driver status, most ably supported by Valerie Domleo, a physicist in the BMC engine development department (later Mrs Donald Morley).

By winning the Criterium des Alpes in 1964 the equipe Rolland and mathematics teacher Augias in their Alfa Romeo Giulia Tubolare Zagato pulled equal with the Morley brothers as the only outright winners in two consecutive years to date. The 2100 mile rally again consisted of three stages, the first of which led from Marseilles to Cannes where 53 of the 73 starters were still in the running. At the second night stop in Chamonix the number was reduced to 36, 9 of them still unpenalized. When the motorcade finally arrived in Monte Carlo, it consisted of 25 cars to be classified, seven of them qualifying for a Coupe des Alpes. In the timed tests six cars had given battle for fastest times of the day, the two Porsche 904s of Günther Klass and Jacques Rey, the Porsche Carrera 2000 of Hans Joachim Walter, the Austin-Healey 3000s of the Morley twins, the 1275 Mini Cooper S cars of Paddy Hopkirk (running in the GT category), and finally the Alfa Romeo Tubolare Zagato of the previous year's winners Jean Rolland/Gabriel Augias. Walter, Klass and Hopkirk all dropped out, leaving the three others well placed for Coupes des Alpes and good overall placings. Immediately behind the outright winner Jean Rolland came the Touring Car winners Vic Elford/David Stone (Ford Cortina GT). He was followed by the Morleys, Aaltonen/Ambrose (1275 Mini Cooper), Jacques Rey/Jean-Pierre Hanrioud (Porsche 904), Erik Carlsson/Gunnar Palm (Saab 850), and John Michael Wadsworth/Peter Cooke (Mini Cooper S), all but Carlsson running in the GT category. The latter's wife, formerly Miss Pat Moss, also drove a Saab but was forced to retire. A Mini Team of the three private entries (Wadsworth, John Gott/William Shepherd, and Margaret Mackenzie/Joe Lowrey) won the Manufacturers' Team Prize for BMC, and Pauline Mayman/Valerie Domleo (970 Mini Cooper S, 13th overall) again received the Coupe des Dames.

In 1965 93 cars were under starter's orders, the highest number seen since 1953. The rally was back on an even keel, and highly thought of by everyone. From the start in Marseilles the more spectacular GT and Prototype cars, such as the Porsche 904s of Jacques Rey, Robert Buchet, Eugen Böhringer/Rolf Wütherich or Pauli Toivonen, dominated in the timed épreuves, challenged only by the Morley's Austin-Healey and Rolland's Alfa Giulia TZ. The previous year's winner, though, soon ran out of road and retired. He was not the only one to disappear, and generally the fast brigade was dwindling faster

Paddy Hopkirk/Ron Crellin in a works Mini Cooper S were the winners of the last genuine French Alpine. Hopkirk took the lead when a three-cornered fight ahead of him ended with the retirement of all three of his rivals.

than the sturdier Touring cars. Only six GT cars arrived at the Grenoble night stop with a clean sheet, among them Buchet, Rey, Morley, and Peter Harper with his Sunbeam Tiger. The best of the Touring cars were not much slower but certainly more robust, so 23 of them were still unpenalized, with Vic Elford (Ford Cortina Lotus) leading that category. Stage 2, Grenoble to Grenoble, reduced the field to 39 cars still running, the GT lead being disputed between Peter Harper (Sunbeam Tiger) and Jean-Pierre Hanrioud (Renault Alpine). Elford ahead of Trautmann (Lancia Flavia) and Timo Mäkinen (Mini Cooper S) was the interim order in the Touring category as the cavalcade took off from Grenoble towards the finish in Monte Carlo. There was to be drama up to, and even beyond, the finish line. Vic Elford retired with a broken distributor on the last of the selective sections, leaving overall victory to René Trautmann/Claudine Bouchet (soon to become Mme. Trautmann) in the Lancia Flavia Zagato. It was a well-deserved win for the Frenchman, who had won four places amongst the top six in the past four years, all for Citroën. Trautmann and seven more Touring cars were awarded Coupes des Alpes, while the only GT car that finished, Peter Harper in a Sunbeam Tiger, was disqualified at scrutineering for undersized valves. The seven other Alpine Cups in the order of general classification were Timo Mäkinen/Paul Easter (Mini Cooper S), Henry Taylor/Brian Melia (Ford Cortina Lotus), Paddy Hopkirk/Henry Liddon (Mini Cooper S), Jean-François Piot/Jean-François Jacob, Jean Vinatier/H Melot (both Renault 8 Gordini), Jean-Claude Ogier/B Ogier (Citroën DS 19), and Tony Fall/Mike Wood (Mini Cooper S). The

winning GT, Bernard Consten/Jean Hébert (Alfa Romeo Giulia TZ) was two minutes late on the road and ninth overall, ahead of the Morleys who were 3 minutes late and five minutes faster in the épreuves than Consten ...

Did this minor incongruity touch off a discussion that lead to a rule change which finally deprived the Coupe des Alpes of its status as the supreme and most soughtafter trophy? The Regulations for 1966 opened the possibility to compensate road penalties for épreuve bonus points. No longer were the winners of Alpine Cups assured that in general classification they would figure above anyone with road penalties. Thus was abandoned a French Alpine tradition strictly respected in 37 rally years. It was revolutionary – and perhaps the ominous writing on the wall ...

But no matter how difficult it was to come to agreements with the authorities over average speeds, itineraries, secret controls and the number of policemen here and there, organizational standards of the French Alpine remained high. Amongst the 81 starters that left Marseilles on their way to Aix-les-Bains, a handful of top drivers in top cars joined battle in the various épreuves of this first stage. Soon the order of Elford (Cortina Lotus), Rolland (Alfa Romeo GTA), Roger Clark (Cortina Lotus) was established, with occasional interference by Hanrioud (Renault-Alpine), Günther Klass (Porsche 911) and Trautmann (Lancia Fulvia Coupé). During the second stage, Aix-les-Bains to Aix-les-Bains, Elford retired with engine trouble, while the last stage saw a frantic attack of the Minis. Hanrioud dropped out with a broken half-shaft, and Trautmann crashed shortly before the finish in Cannes. 19 cars were classified, seven of them unpenalized and due for a Coupe des Alpes. Local hero Jean Rolland, assisted by Gabriel Augias, was once more first in general classification, the only driver with three outright wins in the history of the French Alpine. He was a faithful Alfa Romeo driver, even on the race track which began to interest him more and more. Sadly, he fatally crashed in a Tipo 33 Alfa Romeo during practice for the 1967 Montlhéry 1000 Kilomètres. The Ford versus BMC duel for second place this time went in favour of the Ford Cortina Lotus driven by Roger Clark/Brian Melia, supported by the Franco-Belgian combination of Henri Greder/Gilbert Staepelaere in a similar car, in fifth place. Rauno Aaltonen/Henry Liddon in their Mini Cooper S were third despite two minutes delay on the road, which meant no Coupe des Alpes for the Finn. Jean-François Piot/Jean François Jacob in a Renault R8 Gordini were fourth overall. Despite having lost eleven minutes on the road, the Porsche 911 of Günther Klass/Rolf Wütherich was sixth but had to forego an Alpine Cup. Wütherich, incidentally, had been James Dean's mechanic who, in 1955, survived the legendary actor's fatal crash in a Porsche Spyder.

Three Cup winners had to queue up behind the Cup-less Klass: Noël Labaune/Paul Etienne (Alfa GTA), Lucien Bianchi/Christian Delferrier (Citroën DS 21), and Jean Nicolas/Claude Roure (Renault Gordini). Time for celebrations chez Citroën: its DS 21s also won the Team Prize (Bianchi, R Neyret, Guy Verrier) and the Coupe des Dames (Lucette Pointet/Jacqueline Fougeray).

While there was criticism of the FIA championship system in 1966 and '67 (offering three instead of one championship title), the press had nothing but praise for the organization of the XXVIIIème Critérium International des Alpes held from 4th till 9th September. Its new regulations lumped road penalty points and special test times together. Thus was discarded the old Alpine dogma of the clean sheet as the essential requirement for a Coupe des Alpes. For almost the entire duration of the event it was a three-cornered fight between Gérard Larrousse (Renault Alpine), Mäkinen (BMC Mini

When the Coupe des Alpes opted out of the European Rally Championship, Jean Vinatier/Jean-François Jacob in an Alpine Renault (seen here in 1968) started collecting three Alpine Cups and finally a Gold Cup.

Cooper S), and the very fast Swedish driver Berndt Jansson (Renault Gordini). Dramatically, all three dropped out during the last night. So it was the team of Paddy Hopkirk/Ron Crellin in a group 7 Mini Cooper S, never far behind that trio, which finally scored the outright win. The fabulous Mini had already shone in 1963 and 1965 with second places, plus a third place in 1966. Once again the Works Team paid a heavy price: Fall/Wood and Aaltonen/Liddon had also retired, leaving Hopkirk both as the sole survivor and the outright winner. Runners-up were two Alfa Romeo GTAs driven by Bernard Consten/Peray and Jean-Claude Gamet/Michel Gamet, both – like Hopkirk – with clean sheets. Harry Källström/Gunnar Häggbom (Renault R8 Gordini) in 4th place, however, was two minutes late on the road but, under new rules, became the first ever winner of a Coupe des Alpes with penalty points. Commented *The Autocar:* "The Alpine in its old form is dead, but the four valiant winners of Coupes des Alpes this year will no doubt remember it as the very first of a new series of classic road races."

In those years rallying generally came under heavy criticism as "racing on public roads", which, of course, contained more than a grain of truth. Particularly affected were the rallies extending over more than one country. Some of the countries traversed simply slammed the door in the face of the organizing club. This had already killed the Spa-Sofia-Liège Marathon which was last run in 1964. As a consequence, the AC de

Marseilles et Provence withdrew more and more onto its home ground, the French Alps. Re-shaping its rally caused violent disagreement in the Club Committee and, relying on the halo of the premier French Rally, the organizers now overplayed their hand. Like Le Mans and Indianapolis they felt superior to any FIA Championship, insisting on admitting prototypes to the 1968 and 1969 French Alpine. This meant opting out of the Rally Championship, and they 'broke' the rally in no time. Reduced sponsorship money meant charging horrendously high entry fees. All this proved lethal for the Coupe des Alpes. In the opinion of Peter Browning, last BMC competitions manager and certainly intimately familiar with what went on inside the AC de Marseille, both the works teams and private entrants no longer saw any sense in taking part in that rally. The organizers completely lost contact with the actual rallying scene.

In both years the extremely tough – and expensive – rally was won by Jean Vinatier in a Renault Alpine, also winner each time of a Coupe des Alpes. But internationally, the French Alpine, now outside the Championship, was no longer in the limelight. When Esso withdrew its sponsorship, the 1970 event had to be cancelled. For 1971, however, the Club repented and organized an FIA Championship rally. But it was too late, and the world witnessed the swan song of the Coupe des Alpes. It was financially supported by BP but rumours were afloat that Vinatier and Renault, eager to win the coveted Coupe d'Or for three consecutive Coupes des Alpes, had lobbied strongly for one more edition of the French Alpine Rally. Be that as it may, after three years outside the Championship neither the industry nor private entrants had much confidence left,

and there were only 36 entries. The only serious contenders were the five Renault Alpine cars. Failing to meet the FIA minimum standards of 50 starters, no Championship points were attributed. Bernard Darniche/Alain Mahé won from Jean Vinatier (both Renault-Alpine), with Jean-François Piot third in a Ford Cortina. The desired Coupe d'Or was awarded to Vinatier, but it would be totally wrong to consider his achievement as equivalent to the performances of Ian Appleyard or Stirling Moss.

Here is set out the story of irresistible rise and quick fall of the French Alpine Rally and a great regional French Club that kept alive the grand design first formulated in 1925. It was the idea of conquering all the most famous mountain passes in the Alps, in Austria, France, Germany, Italy, and Switzerland, combining all of these countries into one supreme multi-national trial. This original idea had travelled to the end of the road. By preventing development of a sound new rally concept, in-fighting killed the Coupe des Alpes within a couple of years. The Automobile Club de Marseille et Provence completely vanished from the sporting stage, never to reappear. In 1973 the Marquis de Bretteville laid down the presidency to make way for Etienne Viano, who proposed to rejuvenate the Club Committee, but by that time it was far too late to resurrect the Coupe des Alpes.

Fortunately, however, the idea of a first class Alpine Rally attracting all the major works teams and their star drivers was not dead yet. The comeback of the Alpenfahrt in Austria, its country of origin, gave high-level Alpine Rallying another lease of life for a few years more.

The Austrian Alpine resurrected 1949–1973

At the end of the Second World War Austria lay in ruins. The country regained its independence, albeit with ten years of Allied – including Russian – occupation to follow. By the end of 1945 only 10,000 passenger cars and 18,000 motorcycles were registered in the whole of Austria with a population of 6½ million. In the Soviet-occupied Eastern part of the country, including Vienna, motoring had practically come to a complete standstill. Survival from starvation, not motor sport, was the country's top priority in its programme of reconstruction.

In those critical days the Steyr-Daimler-Puch Company decided not to resume car production, but to concentrate on the manufacture of Steyr trucks and Puch motorcycles. And it so happened that its first works entries in an important international event brought them unexpected glory; the team of three Puch 125 motorcycles won the Team Award in the International Six Days Trial of 1947.

The consequence of this was an understanding between Steyr-Daimler-Puch and the Austrian Automobile, Motorcycle and Touring Club (ÖAMTC, resulting from the postwar merger of the Automobile Club with the Touring Club) to revive motor sport in Austria with the emphasis on motorcycle trials. To crown the planned series of such trials, the Alpenfahrt was to be resumed, with the idea of building it up into a high class training ground for the International Six Days Trial. Thus, in essence, the Austrian Alpine for the next fifteen years was a major motorcycle trial with a minor car rally run parallel with it.

The re-start in 1949 was encouraging. The Alpenfahrt still had sufficient prestige to attract the entry of four Tatra works cars from Czechoslovakia, hot favourites for the event. 48 cars gathered at Zell am See, in the American zone of occupation, to take part in the first postwar Austrian Alpine Rally. The Tatra Team brought its own fuel, mistrusting the Austrian petrol with its octane rating of a mere 56, although a somewhat better quality was made available by the organizers for the event. The brand new aerodynamic rear-engined two litre Tatraplan models contrasted markedly with the rest of the field made up mainly of pre-war cars in varying states of decay. Admittedly, the Swiss contingent was also there with postwar vehicles,

The Czech Tatra team with its aerodynamic two litre Tatraplan saloons dominated the first postwar Austrian Alpine. Josef Chovanec (no. 14) leads the brigade.

Soon after the war Wolfgang Denzel began building sports cars using parts salvaged from wrecked VW Kübelwagens. With this 'Volkswagen ex-WD Equipment' Denzel won the 1100cc sports car class in 1949.

The special 64 VW designed by Ferdinand Porsche for the cancelled 1940 Berlin-Rome event was driven by one-armed Tyrolian Otto Mathé. It retired in 1949 (picture), but won an Austrian Alpine Cup in 1950.

like Max Lindner's Fiat-Simca 1100, Guldemann's MG TC Midget, or Felix Endrich's powerful Gatso sports car built by the Graeco-Dutch rallying ace Maurice Gatsonides. Lt. Vose, US Forces in Austria, was also there with a streamlined pre-war Adler that looked very much like a 'liberated' Le Mans works car of 1937 or 1938.

The few connoisseurs present also took a lively interest in two sports cars fitted with Volkswagen engines, as yet untried in motor sport. One of them was the only surviving example out of a batch of three special Volkswagens (type 64) with streamlined Coupé bodywork designed and built by Ferdinand Porsche in 1939 for the planned Berlin-Rome Race which was never held due to the outbreak of the war. It was driven by the one-armed former motorcycle speedway ace Otto Mathé from Innsbruck but regrettably it soon dropped out. The car actually was the forerunner of the new type 356 Porsche, the production of which had started a few months earlier at the foot of the dreaded Katschberg, in Gmünd through which the rally now passed. It was in Austria's British zone of occupation

that these early Porsche cars were then built in a wooden shed at a rate of five per month.

The other VW-engined sports car could not claim such a pedigree. It was an open four seater initially with wooden bodywork built in Vienna, and called 'Volkswagen WD Equipment'. Driven by Wolfgang Denzel (hence the initials WD) it finished the 1949 Austrian Alpine with a clean sheet and won the 1100cc sports car class, having put up very creditable performances in the timed special tests.

But overall it was the Tatra works cars that dominated the event, with fastest time of the day in the two speed hill climbs going to Karel Vrdlovec (at Katschberg) and Adolf Veřmiřovský (at Pötschen-Pass). Altogether the five class winners were awarded Alpine Cups, with Vrdlovec scoring the highest number of bonus points. He must be considered the outright winner but there was no official general classification. The other class winners (ranked here in accordance with their bonus point account) were Wolfgang Denzel (Volkswagen WD Equipment, sports cars up to 1100cc), Georg Fallenegger

(BMW 327/328, sports cars up to 2000cc), Max Lindner (Fiat-Simca, touring cars up to 1100cc), and Ludwig Breit (Steyr 220, touring cars over 2000cc).

In the absence of the Tatra works cars or other prominent participants from abroad, the 1950 event was based on Velden in Carinthia. There were 56 starters. Fallenegger (BMW 327/28) again won the two litre sports Alpine Cup, but in the 1100cc class this time the winner was Otto Mathé (VW-Porsche type 64), and it was Denzel's turn to retire, with engine trouble. Max Lindner (Simca) was the class winner with the highest number of bonus points and, therefore, the unofficial overall winner of the 1950 Austrian Alpine.

By far the best – and toughest – of the early postwar Austrian Alpines was the 1951 edition, run in cooperation with Allgemeiner Deutscher Automobil Club. No less than 111 cars took off from Kitzbühel, in the Tyrol, to do the first day in the Austrian Alps, and the second day in Bavaria's somewhat less spectacular mountains, a total of 854 miles. The Rally was toughened insofar as there was only one Alpine Cup each for Touring and for Sports cars, regardless of cubic capacity class. The Tatra Team was back in force, and Alois Kopečný won the Alpine Cup for Touring Cars, although Rudolf Smoliner (Lancia Aprilia) would have won general classification on points had there been one. The Sports car Alpine Cup went to German racing and rallying ace Helm Glöckler in a highly tuned Renault 4CV, with Dr Siegfried von Pachernegg class winner in a Denzel 1100. Only 63 cars finished, and 58 of them were classified which is an indication of the event's sporting demands.

In those days the FIA was planning the creation of a European Rally Championship, and at the Austrian Alpine prize giving in Kitzbühel, ÖAMTC secretary general Count Arthur Pachta-Rayhofen was announcing this project with a view of the Austrian Alpine's role in it: "And if one day the great Trials in the Alps will be combined into a (European) Cup, then the Austrian Alpenfahrt with its rich tradition shall, and will be, the finest and toughest in this concert."

Things were to take a different turn, however, but first of all the resurrection of the Austrian Alpine had an animating effect on motor sport in the north westernmost corner of Yugoslavia (now Slovenia), ideal rally territory. Memories of former Alpine Trials were still alive in the area that had been Austrian until 1919. The original pre-Kaiser War Alpenfahrt had passed

through it, and there had been visits by the International Alpine Trial in 1934 as well as by Deutsche Alpenfahrt in 1939.

The result was the creation of a Yugoslav Alpine Rally, or Jugoslovanska Alpska Vožnja, a sprint event of 180 to 250 miles centred round the frightening Vršič (better known under its prewar Italian name of Moistrocca Pass) and the Rovtarica Hill Climb. When it was first held in 1952, Yugoslavia's political situation was precarious, to say the least. The all-powerful Marshal Tito, war-time Communist partisan leader, had broken with Stalin and was still quarrelling both with Italy over Trieste and with Austria over parts of Carinthia. All this did not help to attract a lot of participants from abroad. The Rally was won outright by Alfred Bolz in a Peugeot 203 from Austrian Peter Goritschnig (Chevrolet), while Gert Seibert (Citroën 11 légère), fourth, had put up the fastest time of the day at Rovtarica. Both Seibert and Bolz came from the then independent Saarland (which later reverted to Germany), and they were to become the most faithful clients of the Jugoslovanska Alpska Vožnja. Apart from that they teamed up for the newly created European Rally Championship where they were runners-up in 1953.

By 1953 the political climate had somewhat improved, and more entries were coming in. In the Rovtarica Hill Climb, Mikica Vuković from Belgrade battled with Alex von Falkenhausen for fastest time of the day. Vuković came out the winner in his XK 120 Jaguar, an unusual car for a Yugoslav to own in those days, but he retired soon after this special stage. This left the Rally to Falkenhausen's faithful old BMW 328, with Gert Seibert (Citroën) in second and Austrian Rudolf Smoliner (Lancia Appia) in third place overall. The National Team Award went to the Austrians Karl Hirsch (Lancia Aprilia), Josef Pfundner (Denzel 1100), and Smoliner (Lancia Appia), class winners all three. The Vuković record at Rovtarica only lasted until 1954 when Wolfgang Denzel in his Denzel won the Rally as well as the hill climb from von Falkenhausen.

There was one last Jugoslovanska Alpska Vožnja in 1955 in which Sepp Greger successfully duelled with Kurt Zeller (Porsche 1500 both) for a new Rovtarica record, but the rally was won outright by local hero Dušan Malerič (Porsche 1300). As the Criterium International des Alpes passed through the Yugoslav Alps in 1956 and listed the Yugoslav Automobile Club as co-organizers, there was no need to continue with its own Alpska Vožnja. Full steam ahead, therefore, for the Adriatic

The Yugoslav Alpine was an interesting postwar creation. In 1953 the National Team Prize went to the Austrians (l to r) Trude and Karl Hirsch (Lancia Aprilia), the author and his father Josef Pfundner (Denzel), and Rudi and Gretl Smoliner (Lancia Appia).

Rally (already with FIA European Rally Championship status), an important tourist propaganda instrument for the Dalmatian coast!

Whilst Yugoslavia showed ambitions to partake in motor sport on an international level, Austria in those years concentrated on motorcycle trials and let the car side of the Alpenfahrt decline. ÖAMTC entrusted the event to Karl Basch, a former ISDT Gold Medal winner (1937) soon to be elected an ÖAMTC Vice President. This strong-willed and single-minded man was totally dedicated to the motor bike, without any interest in or knowledge of the four wheeled machines. For 1952 the distance was reduced to less than 700 miles (for a

The Austrian Alpine resurrected 1949-1973

two-day event), participation was down and almost national in character. No less than 38 cars came home with a clean sheet. At its 1952 Autumn Congress in Paris the FIA announced the introduction of the 'European Championship for Touring Car Drivers' for 1953. This was the term originally coined for the

Rally Championship, consisting of ten major international rallies, but Austria did not even submit an application for its Alpine!

For the next five years the distance was round the 900 mile mark, and the organizers' idea of toughness expressed

On her way to the Ladies' Award in the 1954 European Rally Championship, Sheila van Damm (Sunbeam-Talbot 90) scored a class win in the Austrian Alpine.

Karl Hirsch (Lancia Aprilia), winner of Austrian Alpine Cups in 1950 and 1952 (picture), was certainly the shrewdest Austrian rally driver in the early postwar years.

itself on terrible car-breaking road surfaces, almost off-road in character. The higher cylinder capacity classes were given insurmountable handicaps vis-à-vis the small cars, so tiddlers provided the bulk of the field of – on average – 50 cars. Larger touring cars and sports cars were driven away. Foreign entries were few, and came mainly from neighbouring Germany. To add insult to injury, the sidecar motorcycles were sent on their way together with the cars, whilst the itinerary for the solo riders was always selected with remarkable competence.

1954 was an exceptional year, with four works entries from abroad, including the Czech Škoda Team plus Sheila van Damm in a works Sunbeam-Talbot 90. The time schedules were not particularly tough, with the exception of the terrifying Lesachtal section where only five cars came through without loss of marks. Amongst them were two sports cars, Wolfgang Denzel in a Denzel 1300 and Paul Ernst Strähle with his formidable Porsche-engined Volkswagen, baptized 'Tapferle' (Tiny Courageous). Denzel won the Alpine Cup for sports cars.

Although three touring cars made it with clean sheets, no

Alpine Cup for touring cars was attributed, due to an absurdity in the regulations. Sheila van Damm, on her way to the Ladies European Championship title, was late (as were all cars above 1600cc) but she won the unlimited touring car class and the Coupe des Dames.

Instead of rectifying the combined Lesachtal regulations blunder, the same schedule was adopted for 1955, and this time only two drivers managed to come through without any delay. They were Karl Hirsch in a DKW, and Willy Löwinger in a Simca. No Alpine Cups at all were awarded that year.

All this led to a rebellion by the Austrian rally and racing drivers headed by Willy Löwinger. In autumn 1956 a new club was formed, Österreichischer Automobil Sport Club (ÖASC), somewhat similar to the BRDC It marked the beginning of a motor sports boom that culminated with Jochen Rindt's Formula 1 World Championship of 1970. The Alpenfahrt, however, remained unaffected by this new wave of reform for

The Austrian Teddy Quidenus with his powerful Alfa Romeo 1975 was faster than Sheila van Damm in the special tests. However, with her brilliant performance in the dreaded Lesachtal, van Damm won the unlimited touring car class in her Sunbeam Talbot 90.

almost another decade. Suffice to say that Wolfgang Denzel won his third (and last) Austrian Alpine Cup in 1956 driving a large BMW 502 V8 3.2 litre. In a similar car Dr Arnulf Pilhatsch won his first Austrian Alpine Cup in 1957, to repeat category wins in 1959, 1960, 1961, and 1965, to assemble an unprecedented and unrivalled collection of five Austrian Alpenpokale.

Twice in this twilight time the FIA accorded European Rally Championship status on the Austrian Alpine, in 1960 and 1964, and in both cases realized that this decision had been premature, to put it mildly. The 1960 Alpenfahrt saw a battle royal between Eberhard Mahle (Mercedes 220) and René Trautmann (Citroën ID 19) for fastest time of the day in the various special tests, with the German piston manufacturer as the clear winner. The silly regulations, however, so favoured the tiddlers that the two Alpine Cups went to Franz Prach (Steyr-Puch 500, Touring Cars) and Dr Adolf Pilhatsch (BMW 700, GT).

A few hesitant steps towards modernization of the Austrian Alpine set in when, in 1962, one daily stage was run in Yugoslavia, on roads previously included in the former Yugoslovanska Alpska Vožnja. Also, some of the more absurd rules – alien to a modern rally – were being eliminated from the regulations when a second effort was made to establish the Alpenfahrt as a European Championship rally for 1964. With its history dating back to 1910 ÖAMTC now labelled it the 35th Austrian Alpine Rally. Paddy Hopkirk/Henry Liddon in the mighty Austin-Healey 3000 dominated the event from start to finish, with an outright win and the Alpine Cup for GT cars. Precisely 50 years before, Herbert Austin had entered a 3 litre Austin in which his son served as riding mechanic, to win a Silver Medal. Second place (and the touring car Alpine Cup) went to Arnaldo Cavallari/Rubieri (Alfa Romeo), followed by the two Austrian teams of Walter Pöltinger/Erich Werunsky (Morris-Cooper) and Otto Karger/Peter Denzel (Volvo), the latter being Wolfgang Denzel's son. With 46 clean sheets out of a total of 85 starters this was not a difficult rally and the FIA

Dr Arnulf 'Bobby' Pilhatsch won his first Austrian Alpine Cup in 1957 driving a 3.2 litre V8 BMW 502. By 1965 he'd won four more, an absolute record. However, the trophy he cherished most was the Liège-Sofia-Liège Gold Cup for finishing the marathon three years in a row.

Johannes Ortner started his career in the tiny and tremendously noisy Steyr-Puch 500 and 650, winning Alpine Cups in 1961 and 1962 (picture). By 1971 he was an Abarth works driver with two European Hill Climb Championship titles to his credit.

Jochen Rindt (second from right), a twenty year old youngster in his first motor sports season, gave battle to top rally drivers in the 1962 Austrian Alpine driving a Conrero-tuned Alfa Giulietta saloon – until he retired.

Sobieslaw Zasada/Zenon Leszczuk (Porsche 911S) scored an outright win in the 1967 Austrian Alpine. With this car Zasada won yet another European Championship, following his 1966 success in the Steyr-Puch 650 TR.

Paddy Hopkirk accompanied by Henry Liddon completely dominated the 1964 Austrian Alpine in the Austin-Healey 3000. In 1914 Herbert Austin had won a Silver medal in a three litre Austin.

Hannu Mikkola/Anssi Järvi, the Flying Finns in the Lancia Fulvia, were only second in 1968 but Mikkola then switched to a Ford Escort TC to win in 1969.

By 1968 the Austrian Alpine had become attractive for the Scandinavians who began to dominate rallying. Bengt Söderström/ Gunnar Palm in a Ford Escort Twin Cam were the first outright Swedish winners.

Björn Waldegard/Lars Nyström in a works Porsche 911 dominated the 1970 Austrian Alpine. Some years later, in 1979, Waldegard became the first ever Rally World Champion.

felt that there was room for additional improvements. These were effected in 1965 when only 6 cars out of 78 arrived at the finish without loss of marks. So, in his capacity as newly elected member of the International Sporting Commission, this writer managed to bring the 1966 Austrian Alpine back into the European Championship Calendar, to stay there for good.

Once more, Paddy Hopkirk was the outright winner, this time in an Austin Cooper S and assisted by Ron Crellin. They were followed home by the Germans Günther Wallrabenstein/ Ernst Otto Müller (Porsche 911) and Alfred Burkhardt/Otto Koch-Bodes (Ford 20M TS). No one else in the field of 79 starters arrived with a clean sheet. 1966 was also the year when Sobiesław Zasada won the European Rally Championship in the tiny Steyr-Puch 650 TR, giving a tremendous boost to rallying in Austria.

In 1967 the Pole switched to a Porsche 911S, winning the Austrian Alpine on his way to his second championship title. A works Saab V4 driven by Lasse Jönsson/Lasse Ericsson was second, and the Austrians Richard Bochnicek/Günter Pfisterer (Citroën DS 21) third. Asked about the standard of the Austrian Alpine 'Sobek' Zasada, who had taken part with an Alfa Giulia TI in 1963 said: "Four years ago the Alpenfahrt was a pleasure trip. This year it was a tough rally. Yet when selecting the special stages one should aim a little bit at a better road surface."

The event not only counted towards the European Rally Championship but also for the European Rally Trophy for National Teams, an award created by the FIA at the initiative of the Soviet delegation. The Swedish Team composed of two Saabs and one Volvo won the Team Prize in the Alpine; whilst the Austrian National Team captained by Dr Arnulf Pilhatsch (BMW) was awarded the FIA Trophy at the end of the year. The Trophy was not continued in future years.

Sadly, 1967 also saw the last proper French Coupe des Alpes. Luckily this coincided with a drastic reform of the Austrian Alpine, separating cars and motorcycles. The Alpenfahrt was making an effort to regain its almost forgotten status of yesteryear. 1968 saw the introduction of two FIA European Championships of equal importance, one for manufacturers and one for drivers, the Alpenfahrt counting towards the former. It moved its headquarters from Velden in Carinthia (where it had been on 14 occasions) to the

The Austrian Alpine resurrected 1949-1973

Semmering, location of the country's premier hill climb in the years 1899 till 1933. There were 70 starters with a strong contingent of high quality Scandinavians, and works cars from Ford, Lancia, Saab, and Škoda. Bengt Söderström/Gunnar Palm (Ford Escort TC) won the rally after a fierce battle with Hannu Mikkola/Anssi Järvi (Lancia Fulvia HF). Two Austrians duelled for third place, and surprisingly, Walter Roser/Roman Loibnegger (Renault R8 Gordini) were faster than the works BMW 2002 of Dr Arnulf Pilhatsch/Gustav Hruschka, with Alcide Paganelli/Mario Manucci fifth in the second works Lancia Fulvia. For Saab, considered most suitable for the Alpenfahrt, it was a sheer disaster. Carl Orrenius, Stig Blomqvist and Lasse Jönsson dropped out, and Tom Trana/Sölve Andreasson had to be content with 9th place after an 'on-the-roof' excursion into the wilderness. The three Škoda works cars, however, arrived intact, winning the 1150cc class and the team award.

The next year the Alpine Rally was tightened further, the distance from Semmering to Semmering brought up to 1287 miles, including 14 special stages of a total of 112.8 miles. Amongst the 65 starters were many of the world elite. Hannu Mikkola had switched from Lancia to Ford (Escort TC), his partner this time was Mike Wood. His main competitors were championship leaders Harry Källström/Gunnar Häggbom in the Lancia Fulvia HF. To sum it up briefly, Mikkola won 5 special stages, 'Sobek' Zasada/Zenon Leszczuk (Porsche 911S) and Carl Orrenius/Sölve Andreasson (Saab V4) 3 each, Källström 2, and Simo Lampinen/Arne Hertz (Saab V4) one special stage. 18 cars finished, 7 of them with a clean sheet. This gave Mikkola a clear-cut outright win against Källström, with the Saab brigade (Orrenius, Lampinen, and Lasse Jönsson/Lasse Ericsson) occupying places 3 to 5. The 'bus with 150bhp', as the Belgian Gilbert Staepelaere (with André Aerts in the hot seat, runners-up in the 1969 Drivers' Championship behind Källström) described his works Ford 20M RS, scored 6th position, ahead of Richard Bochnicek/Sepp Kernmayer (Citroën DS 21), the best placed Austrians. These seven cars were the only ones with clean sheets. Zasada had to be content with 8th place, his main competitor amongst the GT cars, Joginder Singh, of Safari fame, in another Porsche 911S, had dropped out long ago. Paddy Hopkirk, twice outright winner of the Austrian Alpine, tried his best to make a works Triumph

2.5 PI go fast enough, but clutch failure in the last special stage liberated him from this hopeless mission. Tony Nash was his navigator.

Faced with an ever-increasing number of Rally Championship applications the CSI finally arrived at a sensible solution for 1970. The seven most important European rallies plus the Safari were combined in the International Rally Championship for Makes, while 22 more rallies in Europe constituted a secondary European Rally Championship for Drivers. The Alpenfahrt was included in the prime championship, while two other Austrian events, Semperit-Rally and Rally of the 1000 Minutes, found themselves in the second package. As the country also had its fingers in the pie of two more qualifying events of the Drivers' Championship, Danube Rally (formally Romanian) and Munich-Vienna-Budapest (formally Hungarian), this shows the tremendous role rallying played in Austria in those days.

Not entirely unconnected with this increasing interest was the role that the Porsche Austria Company was now actively taking. The company was run by Ferry Porsche's sister Louise Piech and her son Ernst. One Porsche 911S, two mid-engined Porsche 914/6s, and three 100bhp highly-tuned Volkswagen 1302Ss were entered with Austrian drivers. They were confronted with strong works teams from Ford, Lancia, Porsche, Renault Alpine, and Saab, to cite but the most important. Björn Waldegård/Lars Nyström in a works Porsche 911S immediately took the lead but, miraculously, Austrians Günther Janger/Walther Wessiak (Porsche 914/6) established themselves in second position ahead of many far more famous names. They came to a full stop against a bus, however, and that was the end of great Austrian ambitions. When the 20 survivors arrived at the finish, the order was Waldegård, Hakan 'Bo' Lindberg/Sölve Andreasson (Saab V4), as well as the two Ford Escort Twin Cams of Jean-François Piot/Jean Todt and Britons Adrian Boyd/Dr David Beattie Crawford. Bernard Darniche/Alain Mahé (Renault Alpine) were 5th, ahead of Austrians Walter Lux/Hans Siebert in a Porsche Austria-entered 100bhp Volkswagen, and Franz Wurz/Franz Zögl in another Ford Escort. Only five cars made it with a clean sheet: Waldegård, Lindberg, Piot, Wurz and, remarkably, the one litre class winners Ernst Binder/Erich Streit in the NSU 1000 TTS.

Increased international importance made it imperative

In 1971 Alpine-Renault was the dominant make in the great rallies, and Ove Andersson/Arne Hertz scored a victory in Austria. Not a single driver came home with a clean sheet.

trouble. The remaining 17 special stages went to Alpine, which gave the lead to Thérier until he ran out of road and retired, having scored 7½ 'bests' in special stages. His Alpine colleagues Ove Andersson/Arne Hertz then took over, winning 9½ special stages for an undisputed overall win. The real battle raged behind Ove. Every single driver, including the winner picked up delays; the most punctual at time controls were Dr Fischer (5 minutes), Paganelli and Russling (6 minutes each).

The BMW works cars had endless suspension problems which led to the retirement of Aaltonen/Ron Crellin, while Tony Fall/Mike Wood had perpetual rear axle trouble but nursed the BMW home and into 5th place. In the special stages Fall/Wood featured 16 times amongst the top five. The sole works Lancia (Harry Källström) retired, as did 'Bo' Lindberg in a works Fiat 124 Spider. Alcide Domenico Paganelli in the other Fiat, however, was both fast (ten times amongst the top 5) and wise, to finish second overall behind Andersson, the Swede. The big surprise of this Alpenfahrt was the Porsche Austria-entered Volkswagens. Only their foreign mercenaries, Safari stars Edgar Herrmann and Joginder Singh, hired for publicity, dropped out. The Austrian drivers brought their VWs into third (Klaus Russling/Franz Mikes), fourth (Dr Gernot Fischer/Herbert Kohlweis) and sixth place (Leopold Bosch/Walter Starmann) overall. The team from Salzburg had learnt its lesson and

to find a new location with sufficient hotel capacity. The spa resort of Baden bei Wien, just 15 miles south of Vienna, with its international airport, was selected. The Alpenfahrt was moving closer to where it had started in most instances up until World War II, Vienna. It was the 5th round of the Championship, and Alpine-Renault had already scored 2 wins, in the Monte and the San Remo-Sestriere, giving the blue French cars the lead with 18 points, with Lancia and Nissan with 11 points each. The 1500 mile itinerary contained 18 special stages of 150 miles. Günther Janger in a Porsche Austria-entered 911S left his footprints in the results list with fastest time in the first special stage, one second ahead of Jean-Luc Thérier (Alpine), and 9 seconds faster than Rauno Aaltonen (BMW). Then, less than halfway through the rally, the Austrian retired with suspension

Victory for 'Bo' Lindberg/Helmut Eisendle in the 1972 battle of annihilation with the sturdy Fiat 124 Spyder.

by Harry Källström. Towards the finish it was Günther Janger's turn to win three special stages with the Volkswagen, but all the while one car had calmly stayed within striking distance of those leaders who had won so spectacularly only to lose the rally. Bo Lindberg/Helmut Eisendle in the Fiat 124 Spider won the Alpenfahrt with but one single special stage to their credit. Second place went to Günther Janger/Harald Gottlieb (VW), ahead of Per Eklund/Bo Reinicke (Saab, fastest in one special stage) and Austrians Herbert Grünsteidl/Georg Hopf in yet another Volkswagen. Only eight cars finished the rally.

Three extra-European rounds, the FIA felt, would justify upgrading the series to Rally World Championship. Ten European events were also included, and eight events had been run before the 44th Austrian Alpine. Alpine Renault seemed in an unassailable position with four outright wins, against one each for Datsun, Fiat, Ford, and Saab. All the major works teams were present at the Austrian Alpine, Alpine and Fiat, BMW and Saab, Opel and Toyota, plus the strong Porsche Austria Team, and works-supported Citroëns. Again it was Achim Warmbold (BMW 2002), now most ably supported by Jean Todt, who opened the Alpenfahrt with fireworks. He was fastest in the first six of the 28 special stages, before Bernard Darniche/Alain Mahé (Alpine) could win number 7 for Alpine. Warmbold, however, continued to show his supremacy by bringing his total of best times to twelve. Yet on special stage 12 Warmbold had broadsided the BMW into a milestone which cost not only 25 seconds but also a series of repairs with very awkward consequences. Darniche scored up a total of 8 best

competed on an equal footing with the works cars. The three Škoda 110 L works cars not only won the 1150cc class but were also placed 7th, 8th and 9th. The Škoda brigade was led by its Norwegian stars John Haugland/Arild Antonsen, and supported by the Czechs Oldřich Horsák/Jiří Motal and Milan Zid/Jaroslav Vylit.

Six European rallies as well as Rallye du Maroc, Safari, and the American 'Press on Regardless' now made up the 1972 International Rally Championship. The Alpenfahrt, now with 19 special stages of 205 miles, was the sixth round in the series, and Lancia had almost secured the title. However, things took a different turn in Austria. First of all, the new German star Achim Warmbold won the first four special stages before landing his BMW on its roof which meant retirement. The next special stage went to Rauno Aaltonen in a similar car, and with that BMW had shot its bolts, Tony Fall was also out. Now it was Lancia's turn to attack. Six special stages then went to Simo Lampinen, and Sergio Barbasio supported him with one best time. Then the Lancia threat was over, all three cars were out, Lampinen and Barbasio being preceded

times, while Stig Blomqvist/Arne Hertz won four times before retiring the Saab with a broken differential.

Warmbold's encounter with the milestone resulted in a broken rear suspension radius arm (of a reinforced variety). At the next BMW service point it had to be exchanged for a standard one not quite up to the stress involved in the Alpine, which, again, caused the need for a few more welding jobs. Then, somewhat mysteriously, Warmbold arrived at a time control from the wrong direction. This made Alpine competitions manager Jacques Cheinisse suspicious that something was afoot. His reaction was not altogether straightforward. He borrowed a Citroën hire car from a French journalist, swore him to secrecy, then blocked the route just before Warmbold came through by parking that car across the road. Frantic efforts to remove the obstacle by Warmbold and Ove Andersson/Gunnar Häggbom (Toyota Celica GT) who arrived next on the scene cost some time. At the next time control Warmbold was three, and Andersson one minute late. 25 cars out of the 74 starters arrived in Baden, eight of them with clean sheets. When the rally was over, there were protests and counter-protests. First Warmbold's and Andersson's penalty points were eliminated, bringing the number of clean sheets to ten. Then Warmbold, outright winner ahead of Darniche, was disqualified for having left the prescribed route when approaching the time control from the wrong side. Cheinisse's malpractice still remained in the dark, or was at least unproven. As the case came before the National Court of Appeal, provisional results saw Darniche as the overall winner.

It took a few more weeks, with Jean Todt acting as Sherlock Holmes, until the journalist gave away the secret about his hire car, exposing the rôle of Jacques Cheinisse. Finally, on the initiative of Automobil Club von Deutschland, the case was taken to the FIA International Court of Appeal in Paris. Its verdict reinstated Warmbold/Todt (BMW) as the winner of the 44th Alpenfahrt. This made Darniche second, Per Eklund/Bo Reinicke (Saab) third, Björn Waldegård/Hans Thorszelius (BMW) fourth. Then three Grand Tourers were placed fifth to seventh: Jean-Pierre Nicolas/Michel Vial (Alpine), Bo Lindberg/Helmut Eisendle (Fiat 124 Spider) and the Austrians Klaus Russling/Wolfgang Weiss (Porsche Carrera). Ove Andersson was eighth, ahead of Austrians Herbert Grünsteidel/Georg Hopf (BMW 2002), followed in turn by three of the fast

Salzburg-prepared Volkswagens (1302Ss), driven by Tony Fall/Mike Wood (class winner, 1600 special touring cars) Harry Källström/Claes Billstam and Franz Wittmann/Hans Siebert. The ten unpenalized cars all featured amongst the top dozen, but two drivers with road penalties (Nicolas, 1 minute, and Russling, 2 minutes) were amongst them on account of their superior times in the special stages.

By the time the FIA verdict made these results final the Austrian Alpine was already clinically dead. On 6th October 1973, three weeks after the Alpine, the Yom Kippur War broke out in the Near East. Within 24 hours the oil price soared by 70%, and it continued to rise much further. This was the Oil Shock, with stringent speed limits, driving restrictions, a severe economic recession, and fierce attacks on motoring and motor sport. Environmentalists, forerunners of the Green Movement, joined forces with militant fighters for improved road safety. Rallying was singled out as the worst offender, for wasting energy, polluting the air, endangering 'Brother Tree' in the sacred woods, and for glorifying fast and dangerous driving. In Austria, the long heyday of motor sport ended abruptly, as public opinion changed. Porsche Austria closed its rally department. ÖAMTC, the organizing club, gave in to what was then considered public sentiment. The Alpenfahrt, oldest surviving rally in the world was dead, never to reappear.

Unforgettable Alpine

The magic of the Alpine, however, still survives even though more than thirty years have gone by since the last proper one was held. In Austria, in Switzerland, and in France, no less than five nostalgic or classic Alpines are organized each year, for cars of yesteryear driven, more often than not, by drivers of similar vintage. Two of these historic Alpine Rallies have gone so far as obtaining the status of successor to the original French and Austrian Alpine Rallies respectively.

But that is not all. Way back in 1969 there was a Frazer Nash 'Raid to the Alps' to celebrate the achievements of HJ Aldington. 35 years earlier he had finished his third consecutive International Alpine without loss of marks. To this the Rolls-Royce Enthusiasts Club simply had to reply with its own celebration of former sporting victories. In 1973 it returned to Austria with the 'Great Alpine Commemorative Rally', to

The Austrian Alpine resurrected 1949-1973

Achim Warmbold/Jean Todt in the BMW were fastest in the last Austrian Alpine. They had to wait five months to be announced the winners when the FIA found proof of Cheinisse's most dubious actions.

re-enact the Rolls-Royce triumph of 1913. This Rolls-Royce Rally was repeated in 1993 and in 2003. That year also saw a complete re-run of the Great Austrian Alpine Tour of 1913, open not only to Rolls-Royces but also for other makes of the period. Radley's original 1913 Rolls-Royce Alpine Eagle thus 'competed' against a Minerva, a Praga, a Prince Henry Vauxhall and others of pre-Kaiser War vintage.

In more than six decades, from 1910 till 1973, the Alpine Trials and Rallies have fulfilled their mission to breed motor cars fit for the highest and steepest mountain roads. It was long overdue to recall this important contribution to the development of the modern motor car effected by the original

Alpenfahrt and its many successors. The industry always proudly signalled its achievements in those gruelling tests to the general public by creating new and more attractive special models, beginning with the Austro-Daimler Alpenwagen, the Rolls-Royce Alpine Eagle, and the Audi Alpensieger, via the Delahaye Coupe des Alpes, the Riley Alpine and the Triumph Dolomite, to the Sunbeam Alpine and the Renault Alpine. All this is history now, but the many onlookers at Classic Alpine Rallies simply love to be reminded of the adventures of long ago. It is more than just nostalgia. The aura of the Alpine is indestructible.

Results

THE MAJOR ALPINE TRIALS AND RALLIES

Year	Austria	Italy	International	France	Others
1910	Alpenfahrt	0	0	0	0
1911	Alpenfahrt	0	0	0	0
1912	Alpenfahrt	0	0	0	0
1913	Alpenfahrt	0	0	0	0
1914	Alpenfahrt	0	0	0	Swiss Alpine (CH)
1921	0	Coppa delle Alpi	0	0	0
1922	0	Coppa delle Alpi	0	0	0
1923	Alpenfahrt	Coppa delle Alpi	0	0	Austro-Hungarian Trial (A&H)
1924	0	Coppa delle Alpi	0	0	Alföld-Alpine (A&H) Swiss Alpine (CH)
1925	Alpenfahrt	Coppa delle Alpi	0	0	0
1926	0	GP Montana cancelled	0	0	Austro-Yugoslav Alpine (A&YU) cancelled
1927	0	0	0	0	0
1928	Alpenfahrt	0	1st Intl. Alpine	0	ADAC Reichs- & Alpenfahrt (D)
1929	0	0	2nd Intl. Alpine	0	0
1930	Austr. Alpine Cup	0	0	0	Alföld-Alpine (A & H)
1931	0	0	3rd Intl. Alpine	0	0
1932	0	0	4th Intl. Alpine	1st French	0
1933	Austr. Alpine Cup	0	5th Intl. Alpine	2nd French	0
1934	2 Austr. Alpines	0	6th Intl. Alpine	3rd French	'Ersatz Fuel' Alpenfahrt (A,CH,I)
1935	Alpenfahrt	0	7th Intl. cancelled	4th French	0
1936	0	0	8th Intl. Alpine	5th French	'Ersatz Fuel' Alpenfahrt (CH)
1937	Alpenfahrt	0	0	6th French cancelled	0
1938	0	0	0	7th French	Deutsche Alpenfahrt (D)
1939	0	0	0	8th French	Deutsche Alpenfahrt (D)
1946	0	0	0	9th French	0
1947	0	Stella Alpina	0	10th French	0
1948	0	Stella Alpina	0	11th French	0
1949	Alpenfahrt	Stella Alpina	0	12th French	0
1950	Alpenfahrt	Stella Alpina	0	13th French	0
1951	Alpenfahrt	Stella Alpina	0	14th French	0
1952	Alpenfahrt	Stella Alpina	0	15th French	Yugoslav Alpine (YU)
1953	Alpenfahrt	Stella Alpina	0	16th French	Yugoslav Alpine (YU)
1954	Alpenfahrt	Stella Alpina	0	17th French	Yugoslav Alpine (YU)
1955	Alpenfahrt	Stella Alpina	0	French cancelled	Yugoslav Alpine (YU)
1956	Alpenfahrt	0	0	18th French	0
1957	Alpenfahrt	0	0	French cancelled	0
1958	Alpenfahrt	0	0	19th French	0
1959	Alpenfahrt	0	0	20th French	0
1960	Alpenfahrt	0	0	21stFrench	0
1961	Alpenfahrt	0	0	22nd French	0
1962	Alpenfahrt	0	0	23rd French	0
1963	Alpenfahrt	0	0	24th French	0

Alpine Trials and Rallies 1910 - 1973

Year	Austria	Italy	International	France	Others
1964	35th Alpenfahrt	0	0	25th French	0
1965	36th Alpenfahrt	Alpi Orientali	0	26th French	0
1966	37th Alpenfahrt	Alpi Orientali	0	27th French	0
1967	38th Alpenfahrt	Alpi Orientali	0	28th French	0
1968	39th Alpenfahrt	Alpi Orientali	0	29th French	0
1969	40th Alpenfahrt	Alpi Orientali	0	30th French	0
1970	41st Alpenfahrt	Alpi Orientali	0	French cancelled	0
1971	42nd Alpenfahrt	Alpi Orientali	0	31st French	0
1972	43rd Alpenfahrt	Alpi Orientali	0	French cancelled	0
1973	44th Alpenfahrt	Alpi Orientali1	0	0	0

ALPENFAHRT 1910-1914
Kk Österreichischer Automobil Club, start & finish in Vienna

Year/ date	Distance	Starters	Classified	0 points lost	Overall winner
1910 26/29 June	867km	15	6	6	Count Alexander Kolowrat (A), Laurin & Klement; Count Paul Draskovich (A), Laurin & Klement; Otto Hieronimus (A), Laurin & Klement; Robert Koch (A), Opel; John Diehle (D), NAG; Louis Obruba (A), Mathis. Team Prize: Laurin & Klement: Count Alexander Kolowrat (A), Count Paul Draskovich (A), Otto Hieronimus (A).
1911 13/16 May	1421km	51	41	12	Eduard Fischer (A), Austro-Daimler; Ferdinand Porsche (A), Austro-Daimler; Count Heinrich Schönfeldt (A), Austro-Daimler; Nikolaus von Popowicz (A); Austro-Daimler; Severin Schreiber (A), Austro-Daimler); Karl Vitak (A), NAG; Fritz Hückel (A), Nesselsdorf; Hans Ledwinka (A), Nesselsdorf; Valentin Kadlczik (A) [Driver Bush [GB]], Coventry-Daimler; Otto Hieronimus (A), Laurin & Klement; Robert Deutsch (A), Puch; August Horch (D), Audi. Team Prize: Austro-Daimler: Eduard Fischer (A), Ferdinand Porsche (A), Count Heinrich Schönfeldt (A).
1912 16/23 June	2364km	85	72	25	Prince Elias of Parma (A), Austro-Daimler; Count Heinrich Schönfeldt (A), Austro-Daimler; Ferdinand Porsche (A), Austro-Daimler; Archduke Karl Franz Josef (A), Austro-Daimler; Giovanni Marcellino (I/A), Fiat; Karl Bettaque (A), Fiat; Prince Alexander Croy (A), Fiat; Fritz Opel (D), Opel; Robert Koch (A), Opel; Carl Joerns (D), Opel; Jean Pfanz (D), Benz; Otto Philipp (D), Benz; Max Lauffer (A), Benz; Hermann Lange (D), Audi; Alexander Graumüller (D), Audi; Karl Dobner von Dobenau (A), Gräf & Stift; Karl Köhler (D), Hansa; Count Alexander Kolowrat (A) [Driver Otto Hieronimus (A)], Laurin & Klement; Louis Obruba (A), Mathis; Willy von Gutmann (A), Mercedes; Sylvain de Jong (B), Minerva; Franz Seidel (A), NAG; Johann Sirutschek (A), Praga; Heinrich Luksch (A), RAF; Franz Fuchs (A), WAF. 2 Team Prizes (ex aequo): Opel: Fritz Opel (D), Robert Koch (A), Carl Joerns (D). Fiat: Giovanni Marcellino (I/A), Karl Bettaque (A), Baron Hans von Veyder-Malberg (A).
1913 22/29 June	2650km	43	31	9	Curt Cornelius Friese (A), Rolls-Royce; Sylvain de Jong (B), Minerva; Georg Paulmann (D), Horch; Count Alexander Kolowrat (A) [Driver Otto Hieronimus (A)], Laurin & Klement; Walter Delmár (H), Benz; Johann Sirutschek (A), Raaba; Hermann Lange (D), Audi; Alexander Graumüller (D), Audi; Louis Obruba (A), Audi.

Year/date	Distance	Starters	Classified	0 points lost	Overall winner
1914 14/23 June	2931km	75	50	19	**Team Prize: Audi:** August Horch (D), Hermann Lange (D), Alexander Graumüller (D). Baron Wladimir Steinheil (A), Gräf & Stift; James Radley (GB), Rolls-Royce; Count Alexander Kolowrat (A), Laurin & Klement; Walter Delmár (H), Benz; Josef Zák (A), Praga; August Horch (D), Audi; Alexander Graumüller (D), Audi; Hermann Lange (D), Audi; Louis Obruba (A), Audi; Robert Muhri (A), Audi; Franz Henschel (A), Austro-Daimler; Prince Elias of Parma (A), Austro-Daimler; Anton Czech (A), Austro-Daimler; Martin Schneeweiss (A), Fiat; Giovanni Marcellino (I/A), Fiat; Karl Bettaque (A), Fiat; Sylvain de Jong (B), Minerva; Karl von Klinkosch (A), Minerva; Robert Koch (A), Opel. **2 Team Prizes (ex aequo): Audi:** August Horch (D), Hermann Lange (D), Alexander Graumüller (D). **Hansa:** Albin Kappel (D), Ing Garais (D), Karl Köhler (D).

In 1914 the Great Alpine Challenge Trophy was definitely awarded to the competitor with the smallest number of penalty points accumulated in 1912, 1913, and 1914. It was won ex-aequo by the following five, all of them with clean sheets in all three years: Alexander Graumüller, Audi; Sylvain de Jong, Minerva; Count Alexander Kolowrat, Laurin & Klement; Hermann Lange, Audi; Louis Obruba, Mathis and Audi.

AUSTRIAN ALPINE TRIALS 1923-1937
Österreichischer Automobil Club

Year/date	Name	Start & finish	Distance	Starters	Classified	0 points lost	Overall winner
1923 22/27 June	Gesellschafts-Alpenfahrt	Vienna-Salzburg	950km	15	?	not applicable	Count Rudolf Kinsky (A), Steyr 3.3 litre
1925 20/28 June	Österreichische Alpenfahrt	Vienna-Munich	2280km	41	17	4	Count Heinrich Schönfeldt (A), Steyr VII Team Prize: Steyr: Walter Delmár (H), Count Heinrich Schönfeldt (A), Baron Leo Haan (A)
1928 23/24 June	Alpenländische Kartellfahrt	Klagenfurt-Graz	800km	33	?	18	Josef Sigl (A), Gräf & Stift 78 litre
1930 14/17 June	Fahrt um den Österr. Alpenpokal	Vienna-Bregenz	1272km	36	29	9	Desiderius von Bitzy (A), Austro-Daimler 3 litre Team Prize: Praga: Jaroslav Heussler (CS), Karl Matuschovsky (CS), Anton Suldowsky (CS)
1933 24/25 June	Fahrt um den Österr. Alpenpokal	6 Start & Finish Points	variable	42	34	21	No General Classification Team Prize: Austro-Daimler: Desiderius von Bitzy (A), Richard Gerin (A), Anton Czech (A)
1934 16/17 June	Fahrt durch die Österr. Alpen	Vienna-Vienna	maximum 1981km	37	35	30	No General Classification, no Alpine Cup offered 2 Team Prizes (ex aequo): Steyr: Count Ludwig Lodron (A), Ernst Rausch (A), August Picmaus (A) Standard: Count Peter Orssich (A), Hans Georg Koch (A), Adolf Fröhlich (A)

Alpine Trials and Rallies 1910 - 1973

Year/date	Name	Start & finish	Distance	Starters	Classified	0 points lost	Overall winner
1934 6/7 Oct	Österreichische Höhenstraßenfahrt	Schottwien-Semmering	maximum 1360km	15	9	not applicable	Ernst Rausch/Rudolf Zikesch (A), Steyr 100
1935 29/30 June	Österreichische Höhenstraßenfahrt	Vienna-Semmering	maximum 1917km	17	14	9	No General Classification, no Alpine Cup offered.
1937 17/19 July	Österreichische Alpenfahrt	Baden-Baden	1900km	38	17	7	Fritz Huschke von Hanstein (D), Hanomag Team Prize: Hanomag: Frau Christl Meinecke (D), Huschke von Hanstein (D), Wilhelm Scholle (D)

ALFÖLD-ALPENFAHRT 1923-1930
Österreichischer Automobil Club & Királyi Magyar Automobil Club

Year/date	Start & finish	Distance	Starters	Classified	0 points lost	Overall winner
1923 11/16 June	Vienna-Budapest	1795km	39	27	12	Walter Delmár (H), Steyr
1924 14/21 June	Budapest-Vienna	2150km 1900km	48	37	21	Touring Cars: Baron Hans von Veyder-Malberg (A), Austro-Daimler, ex aequo with Count Ulrich Kinsky (A), Steyr Small Cars: Franz Bittmann (CS), Tatra, ex aequo with Josef Vermirovský (CS), Tatra Team Prize Touring Cars: Steyr: Walter Delmár (H), Ladislaus von Almasy (H), Count Heinrich Schönfeldt (A) Team Prize Small Cars: Tatra: Josef Vermirovský (CS), Franz Bittmann (CS), Josef Cservenka (CS)
1930 10/13 July	Vienna-Budapest	1320km	40	27	15	Laszlo Balazs (H), Magosix 2 Team Prizes (ex aequo): Austro-Daimler: Desiderius von Bitzy (A), Philipp von Schoeller (A), Count Felix Spiegel (A), Gräf & Stift: Josef Gräf (A), Franz Pauker (A), Ad Stern (A) [driver Gustav Schimatzek,(A)]

COUPE INTERNATIONALE DES ALPES 1928-1936
(Jointly organized by up to 7 National Automobile Clubs)

N°	Year/date	Start/finish	Distance	Starters	Classified	Un-penalized	Alpine Cups (teams)	
1st	1928 12/18 Aug	Milan-Munich	1964km	86	44	not applicable	4: Adler:	Otto Löhr (D), André Dewald (D), Hans Coenen (D) Brennabor: Fritz Backasch (D), Hans Niedlich (D), Fritz Lehnert (D)
							Minerva:	Leopold Roger (B), René van Parys (B), Edgar Goujon (B)
							OM:	Giuseppe Morandi (I), Vincenzo Coffani (I), Antonio Masperi (I)

N° Year/ date	Start/ finish	Distance	Starters	Classified	Un-penalized	Alpine Cups (teams)	
2nd 1929 7/11 Aug	Munich-Milan/Como	2518km	80	48	not applicable	2: Hansa:	Fredo Sporkhorst (D), Ernst Werner Sporkhorst (D), Eduard Hörbe (D) BMW: Max Buchner (D), Albert Kandt Jr (D), Willy Wagner (D)
1930	no International Alpine Trial held						
3rd 1931 30 Jul/6 Aug	Munich-Berne	2364km	62	44	8	2: Praga:	Jaroslav Heussler (CS), St Pavlovsky (CS), Anton Suldowsky (CS)
						Wanderer:	Alexander Graumüller (D), Bernhard Bau (D), Hans Hinterleitner (D)
4th 1932 28 Jul/4 Aug	Munich-San Remo	2598km	99	87	34	4: Talbot:	Hon. Brian Lewis (GB), Tim Rose-Richards (GB), Norman Garrad (GB)
						Wanderer:	Alexander Graumüller (D), Bernhard Bau (D), Hans Hinterleitner (D)
						Tatra:	Hans Schicht (CS), Wolfgang von Mayenburg (CS), Fr Hoffmann (CS)
						Riley:	Victor Leverett (GB), Charles Riley (GB), G Dennison (GB)
5th 1933 31 Jul/4 Aug	Merano-Nice	1920km	121	95	3	5: Ford:	N Went/Janus van der Kamp (NL), Dr JJ Sprenger van Eyk/Paul Lamberts Hurrelbrinck (NL), AAJ Wieleman/J Jansen (NL)
						Hotchkiss:	WF Bradley (GB), Duhamel/Buzzi (F), Louis Gas/Jean Trevoux (F)
						Adler:	Friedrich Karl Widenmann/Fischer (D), Philipp Hoffmann/Wulff (D), Adolf Max Gehrmann/Matiasek (D)
						Riley:	Charles Riley/E Maher (GB), J Ridley/FJ Millington (GB), TC Griffiths/W Greenway (GB)
						MG:	Tommy Wisdom/Mrs Elsie Wisdom (GB), WC Watkinson/HA Ward Jackson (GB), L Welch/DF Welch (GB)
6th 1934 7/12 Aug	Nice-Munich	2900km	127	94	67	8: Adler Trumpf:	Paul von Guilleaume/Fritz Poensgen (D), Rudolf Hasse/Karl Artz (D), Otto Löhr/Willy Herrmann (D)
						BMW:	Richard Brenner/Werberger (D), Albert Kandt Jr/Koch (D), Ernst von Delius/Leidenberger (D) Delahaye: Albert Perrot/Honard (F), Marcel Dhôme/Jeanneaux (F), Robert Girod/Denot (F)
						Opel:	Heinrich Diehl/Johann Appel (D), Alex Blüm/Karl Treber II (D), Franz Traiser/Georg Waldhaus (D)
						Talbot:	Tommy Wisdom/Mrs Elsie Wisdom (GB), W Couper/Day (GB), Hugh Eaton/Higgins (GB)
						Triumph:	Claude Vivian Holbrook/Shemans (GB), J Ridley/Sharp (GB), Victor Leverett/Rollason (GB)
						Wanderer:	Count Max Sandizell/Schmutz (D), Karl Friedrich Trübsbach/

Alpine Trials and Rallies 1910 - 1973

N° Year/ date	Start/ finish	Distance	Starters	Classified	Un-penalized	Alpine Cups (teams)	
						Adler	Franz Kosel (D), Wilhelm Kraemer/Alfred Schade (D)
						Diplomat:	Günther Wimmer/Wulff (D), Adolf Max Gehrmann/ Schneider (D), Philipp Hoffmann/Wahl (D)
7th 1935 5/9 Aug	Cancelled						
8th 1936 20/27 Aug	Lucerne-Interlaken	2.342km	72	64	23	4: DKW:	Fritz Trägner/Erwin John (D), Alfred Weidauer/Kurt Lehmann (D), Wilhelm Kraemer/Otto Munzert (D)
						Adler:	Paul von Guilleaume/ von Uhrich (D), Rudolph Sauerwein/Wilhelm Kramer (D), Count Peter Orssich/ Willy Hermann (A/D)
						Ford:	AP van Strien/J Langelaan (NL), Karel Ton/Frits Diepen (NL), Jan Erens/J Krabbenboo (NL)
						Hanomag:	Karl Haeberle/Friedrich Bund (D), Wilhelm Glöckler/ Fritz de Bucourt (D), Georg Roericht/Franz Glombik (D)

Of all the 29 Alpine Cups awarded to teams, Adler won 5, Wanderer 3, BMW, Ford, Riley and Talbot 2 each, and one Alpine Cup went to the following makes: Brennabor, Delahaye, DKW, Hanomag, Hansa, Hotchkiss, MG, Minerva, OM, Opel, Praga, Tatra, and Triumph.

ALL GLACIER CUP WINNERS 1928-1936

1928 (19):   WR Wittich (D), Mercedes; Dr Robert Krailsheimer (D), Mercedes; Fritz von Zsolnay (A), Gräf & Stift; Paul von Guilleaume (D); Steyr; EW Sporkhorst (D), Hansa; Johann Hinterleitner (D), Hupmobile; Carl Deilmann Jr (D), Austro-Daimler; Hans Georg Koch (A), Standard; Mic Ryffel CH), Peugeot; Vaccarossi (I), Lancia; Ernst Kotte (D), Simson; Dr Oskar Schmidt (A), Talbot; Schiaffino (I); Alfa Romo; Baragiola (I), Alfa Romeo; Gino Crespi (I); Fiat; Marchese Gian Maria Cornaggia Medici (I), Fiat; Mariani (I), Fiat; Stohanzel (CS), ZET; Leo Karger (CS), ZET.

1929 (36):   Georg Kimpel (D), Mercedes; Wilhelm Merck (D), Mercedes; Dr Robert Krailsheimer (D), Mercedes; Alfred Hirte Jr (D), Mercedes; Edgar Bieber (D), Mercedes; Karl Schwabe (D), La Salle; Otto Merz (D), Mercedes; Rudolf Caracciola (D), Mercedes; Paul Bartmann (D), Hupmobile; G von Natzmer (D), Stoewer; Carlo Salamano (I), Fiat; Cesare Pastori (I), Fiat; Alessandro Valagna (I), Ford; U Appolonia (I), Ford; P Messerli (CH), Ford; E Reguzzi (CH), Ford; Theodor Rosthoff (D), Ford; Carl von Guilleaume (D), Chevrolet; Emilio Ricchetti (I), Bugatti; Desiderius von Bitzy (A), Austro-Daimler; Fritz Backasch (D), Brennabor; Fritz Lehnert (D), Brennabor; Christian Werner (D), Mercedes; Alfred Gutknecht (D), Wanderer; Hermann Atmer (D), Wanderer; Karl Kappler (D), Wanderer; Alexander Graumüller (D), Wanderer; Dr Fritz Hetzel (D), Wanderer; Herbert Rüedi (CH), Lancia; Walter Jähnig (D), Hansa; Alberto Dosio (I), OM; Mrs Tilly Kotte (D), Simson; Riella (I), Alfa Romeo; F Brambilla (I), Alfa Romeo; Hellmuth Butenuth (D), Hanomag.

1930:   No International Alpine Trial held

1931 (11):   Donald Healey (GB), Invicta; Walter Delmár (H), Mercedes; Desiderius von Bitzy (A), Austro-Daimler; Count Felix Spiegel-Diesenberg (A), Austro-Daimler; Philipp von Schoeller (A), Austro-Daimler; Humfrey E Symons (GB), Clément-Talbot; EH Scholten (CH), Lancia; Carlo Adorno (I), OM; Hellmuth Butenuth (D), Hanomag; Carl Pollich (D), Hanomag; Frau Liliane Roehrs (D), Hanomag.

1932 (25):   Charles M Needham GB), Invicta; A Lace (GB), Invicta; Donald Healey (GB), Invicta; EH Scholten (CH), Lancia; Dr Armand Lettich (A), Fiat; Jacques van der Meulen (NL), Ford; J Sprenger van Eyk (NL), Ford; C Siddeley (GB), Armstrong Siddeley; WF Bradley (GB), Armstrong-Siddeley; H Symons (GB), Armstrong-Siddeley; Hans Joachim Bernet (D), Wanderer; Karl Kappler (D), Wanderer; Rudolph Sauerwein (D), Bugatti; Walter Delmár (H), Bugatti; Dr Adolf Noll (D), Austro-Daimler; W Couper (GB),

Lagonda; A Gripper (GB), Frazer Nash; Harold John Aldington (GB), Frazer Nash; Miss Katherine Martin (GB), Wolseley; Miss Margaret Allen (GB), Wolseley; WC Watkinson (GB), MG; Dr Otto Enoch (D), Hanomag; Jack Hobbs (GB), Riley; Roy Franey (GB), Riley; Eric W Deeley (GB), Singer, GMD Maltby (GB), Riley; C Montague-Johnstone (GB), Riley.

1933 (2): Walter Delmár (H), Bugatti; René Carrière/Henry Avril (F), Alfa Romeo.

1934 (35): RL Richardson/Ranger (GB), Railton; E Mutsaerts/A Kouwenberg (NL), Ford; A van Strien/Carol Schaade (NL), Ford; N Flisette/Weber (NL), Ford; S Posthumus/van der Mark (NL), Ford; B Neamtu/Frumusanu (R), Ford; R Getac/Hugo Dreyer (CH), Ford; Jean Trevoux/Buzzi (F), Hotchkiss; J von Biro/von Pucher (H), Bugatti; Gaston Descollas/Mme Claire Descollas (F), Bugatti; Mrs Lucy Schell-O'Reilly/Laury Schell (US), Delahaye; D Davids/Frans Habnit (NL), Railton; René Carrière/Henry Avril (F), Hotchkiss; Miss Edith Frisch/Karl Treber I (D), Opel; Willy Engesser/Arthur Engesser (D), Opel; Baron von Goldegg/Dobias (CS), Alfa Romeo; Rudolph Sauerwein/Becker (D), Adler; Walter Delmár/Benedek (H), Adler; Arthur von Mumm/Klein (D), Röhr; H Aldington/Neil Berry (GB), Frazer Nash; John Tweedale/Holden King (GB), Frazer Nash; Peter Cadbury/Anthony Heal (GB), Aston Martin; T Clarke/Yeldham (GB), Aston Martin; Count Felix Spiegel-Diesenberg/Wolfgang Brandauer (A), BMW; Alfred Gutknecht/Ernst Voigtländer (D), BMW; Frau Liliane Roehrs/Rembach (D), BMW; Count Peter Orssich/Frau Mühlbacher (A), Standard; H Symons/W Harold Rees (GB), MG; Capt OH Frost/Beckett (GB), Lancia; Maurice Newnham/S Holbrook (GB), Triumph; Donald Healey/Pearce (GB), Triumph; Paul Schweder/Frau Emma Schweder (D), Adler; R Gardner/Belve (GB), Singer; F Stanley Barnes/James Donald Barnes (GB), Singer; Ian Ferguson Connell/Hall (GB), Singer.

1935: Cancelled

1936 (17): Gerard Bakker Schut/G Buddemeyer (NL), Lincoln Zephyr; DH Davids/Paul Lamberts Hurrelbrinck (NL), Ford; Cloppenburg/Weinberger (D), Ford; Oscar Bally/H Meier (CH), Talbot; Günther Wimmer/Heinrich Ziervogel (D), Adler; T Wisdom/Mrs Elsie Wisdom (GB), SS Jaguar; Baron Carl Adam Aretin/Frau Eugenie von Plessen (D), BMW; Baron Günther Egloffstein/Baroness Herta Egloffstein (D), BMW; Alfred Gutknecht/Rolf Bruns (D), BMW; Friedrich Holzhäuer/Hugo Paechter (D), BMW; Donald Healey (GB), Triumph; Hugo Meffert/Josef Maier (D), BMW; Alfred Schmidt/Karl Gräfe (D), BMW; Paul Lein/Waldemar Rühling (D), DKW; Karl Lindner/Alfred Hanzig (D), DKW; Ernst Mäurich/Georg Sieger (D), DKW; Dr Reinhart Siebert/Jakob Keul (D), DKW.

SWISS ALPINE TRIAL 1924
Automobil Club der Schweiz

Year/date	Overall winner
1924 7/12 July	Fritz Nallinger (D), Benz
	Team Prize: Minerva: Sylvain de Jong (B), Edgar Goujon (B), Marmini (I)

DEUTSCHE ALPENFAHRT 1938-1939
Oberste Nationale Sportbehörde (ONS)

Year/date	Start/finish	Distance	Starters	Classified	Not penalized	Alpine Cups (category winners)
1938 28/30 July	Innsbruck/ Vienna	1672km	117	82	67	Fritz Roth (D), BMW 328 (sports cars) Edgar Kittner (D), Opel Olympia (touring cars)
1939 31 July/2 Aug	Munich/ Vienna	1627km	141	122	45	Fritz Roth (D), BMW 328 (sports cars) Edgar Kittner (D), Opel Olympia (touring cars)

Alpine Trials and Rallies 1910 - 1973

RALLYE DES ALPES FRANÇAISES 1932-1971
(also Rallye International des Alpes and Critérium International des Alpes)
Automobile Club de Marseille et Provence, Start & finish 1932-1936 Marseilles
With the exception of 1968/69 all rallies from 1953 onwards were European Rally Championship events.
In 1971 no points were attributed due to an insufficient number of starters.

N° Year	Distance	Class winners
1. 1932 14/15 July	? km	René Carrière (F), Alfa Romeo (over fr 50.000); Dupré (F), Chevrolet (up to fr 50.000); Laurent (F), Rallye (up to fr 40.000); Albert Rousset (F), Renault (up to fr 30.000); Mlle Sajous (F), Mathis (up to fr 30.000)
2. 1933	? km	Edouard Legré (F), Bugatti (over fr 70.000); Guérin (F), Panhard (up to fr 70.000); Dr Marc Angelvin (F), Renault (up to fr 50.000); Fernand Michel (F), Citroën (up to fr 30.000); Gaston Descollas (F), Amilcar (up to fr 20.000)
3. 1934	? km	Gaston Descollas (F), Bugatti (over fr 70.000); Ernest de Regibus (F), Delahaye (up to fr 70.000); Tasso (F), Hotchkiss up to fr 50.000); Péguret (F), Ford (up to fr 40.000); Charles Roch (F), Ford (up to fr 30.000); Reybert (F), Renault (up to fr 20.000)
4. 1935 13/15 July	969km	Gaston Descollas (F), Bugatti (coefficient over 200); Albert Perrot (F), Delahaye (up to 200); Charles Roch (F), Amilcar (up to 100); Reybert (F), Renault (up to 60); Maurice Pupil (F), Fiat (up to 30)
5. 1936 14/16 Aug.	1304km	René Carrière (F), Matford (over 3000 cc); Pfister (F), Citroën (3000 cc); Guy Lapchin (F); Riley (1500 cc); Trophée des Alpes Françaises: Charrier (F), Renault (over fr 20.000); Dr L Billon (F), Renault (up to fr 20.000)
6. 1937	Cancelled	

N° Year/date	Marseilles to:	Countries traversed	Distance km	Starters	Classified	Alpine Cups	Alpine Cup winners
7th 1938 14/17July	Marseilles	F	1500	26?	17	2	Count Heinrich von der Mühle/Frau Eugenie von Plessen (D), BMW 328; M & Mme Gaston Descollas (F), Lancia Aprilia.
8th 1939 14/16July	Marseilles	F	1215	36	19	2	Wolfgang Denzel/Hubert Stroinigg (A), BMW 328; Mme Claire Descollas (F), Lancia Aprilia.
9th 1946 12/15July	Marseilles	F	1050	37	11	0	–
10th 1947 13/16July	Cannes	F	1665	61	27	2	André Clermont (F), Lancia Aprilia; Gaston Descollas (F), Bugatti.
11th 1948 14/17July	Nice	F,CH	1873	71	29	8	Ian Appleyard/Dr Dick Weatherhead (GB), Jaguar SS 100; Leonard Potter/C Alan May (GB), Allard K-type; George Murray-Frame/L J Onslow Bartlett (GB), Sunbeam-Talbot; Gaston Gautruche/Claude Mazalon (F), Citroën 11; M & Mme Gaston Descollas (F), Lancia Aprilia; Georges Claude/Pierre Clause (F), Lancia Aprilia; Robin Richards/John Beaumont (GB), HRG; Freddy & Valentine Auriach (F), Simca 8.
12th 1949 13/21July	Nice	F,CH,I	2946	94	31	1	Gaston Gautruche (F), Citroën 11.
13th 1950 12/21July	Cannes	F,CH,I,A	3200	95	38	7	Ian & Pat Appleyard (GB), Jaguar XK 120; Edmond Signoret/Elie Guibourdenche (F), Dyna-Panhard; Guy Lapchin/Charles Plantivaux (F), Dyna-Panhard; Jean-Paul Colas/Michel Canello (F), Dyna-Panhard; J Masset/Louis Pons (F), Dyna-Panhard; Michel Grosgogeat/

N° Year/date	Marseilles to:	Countries traversed	Distance km	Starters	Classified	Alpine Cups	Alpine Cup winners
14th 1951 11/20 July	Cannes	F,CH,I,A	3207	65	28	10	Biagini (F), Dyna-Panhard; Dolf Burgerhout/Henk Sijthof (NL), Dyna-Panhard. François & Mireille Landon (F), Renault 4CV; Dr Marc & Nicole Angelvin, (F), Simca; John Gott/Jock Gillespie (GB), HRG; George Duff/Eric Winterbottom (GB), Frazer Nash; Roberto Piodi (I), Lancia; Tommy Wisdom/Mrs Elsie Wisdom (GB), Aston-Martin; Edgar Wadsworth/Cyril Corbishley (GB), Healey; Ian & Pat Appleyard (GB), Jaguar XK 120; Rolf Habisreutinger/Walo Hörning (CH), Jaguar XK 120; Godfrey Imhoff/ R Robertson (GB), Cadillac-Allard.

N° Year/date	Marseilles to:	Countries	Distance traversed km	Starters	Classified	Alpine Cups	Overall Winner, 1st General Classification
15th 1952 11/17 July	Cannes	F,I,A,CH	3291	85	23	10	Baron & Baroness Alex von Falkenhausen (D), BMW 328
16th 1953 10/16 July	Cannes	F,I,A,D,CH	3089	101	54	25	Helmut Polensky/Walter Schlüter (D), Porsche
17th 1954 9/16 July	Cannes	F,I,A,D,CH	3563	79	37	11	Wolfgang Denzel/Hubert Stroinigg (A), Denzel
1955	Cancelled						
18th 1956 6/13 July	Marseilles	F,I,YU	4103	83	34	17	Michel Collange/Robert Huguet (F), Alfa Giulietta
1957	Cancelled						
19th 1958 4/12 July	Marseilles	F,I,CH	3150	58	25	7	Bernard Consten/Roger de Lageneste (F), Alfa Giulietta
20th 1959 23/29 June	Cannes	F,I,A	3840	59	27	9	Paul Condriller/Georges Robin (F), Renault Dauphine
21st 1960 26/30 June	Cannes	F,I,CH	3010	65	39	6	Roger de Lageneste/Henri Gréder (F), Alfa Giulietta
22nd 1961 24/28 June	Cannes	F,I,CH	2990	66	25	1	Donald Morley/Erle Morley (GB), Austin-Healey
23rd 1962 16/21 June	Cannes	F,I	4057	48	28	5	Donald Morley/Erle Morley (GB), Austin-Healey
24th 1963 20/25 June	Marseilles	F,CH,I	3793	78	24	6	Jean Rolland/Gabriel Augias (F), Alfa Giulietta
25th 1964 23/28 June	Monaco	F,CH,I	3380	73	25	7	Jean Rolland/Gabriel Augias (F), Alfa Giulia TZ
26th 1965 19/25 July	Monaco	F,CH,I	3520	93	22	8	René Trautmann/Mme Claudine Bouchet (F), Lancia Flavia
27th 1966 5/10 Sept	Cannes	F	3.990	80	19	7	Jean Rolland/Gabriel Augias (F), Alfa Romeo GTA
28th 1967 4/9 Sept	Menton	F	3704	79	15	4	Paddy Hopkirk/Ron Crellin (EIR/GB), Mini Cooper S
29th 1968 2/7 Sept	Juan les Pins	F	3790	64	12	3	Jean Vinatier/Jean-François Jacob (F), Renault-Alpine
30th 1969 1/6 Sept	Juan les Pins	F	3740	70	41	6	Jean Vinatier/Jean-François Jacob (F), Renault-Alpine
31st 1970	Cancelled						
32nd 1971 21/26 June	Marseilles	F	2340	34	11	2	Bernard Darniche/Alain Mahé (F), Renault-Alpine

ALL COUPE DES ALPES WINNERS 1952-1971
(arranged in the order of General Classification)

1952 (10):   Baron & Baroness Alex von Falkenhausen (D), BMW 328; Maurice Gatsonides/George Samworth Jr (NL/US), Jaguar XK 120; Ernest de Regibus/Pierre Chaix (F), Renault 4CV; Ian & Pat Appleyard (GB), Jaguar XK 120; René Fabre/Jacques Fabre (F), Dyna Panhard;

Louis Picon/Turquetil (F), Renault 4CV; Ferdinando Gatta/Jacques Ickx (I/B), Lancia Aurelia B20; George Murray-Frame/John Pearman (GB), Sunbeam-Talbot 90; Mike Hawthorn/'Chippy' Chipperton (GB), Sunbeam-Talbot 90; Stirling Moss/John Cutts (GB), Sunbeam-Talbot 90.

Coupe d'Or: Ian Appleyard (GB), Jaguar.

1953 (25): Helmut Polensky/Walter Schlüter (D), Porsche1500; Rudolf Sauerwein/Max Nathan (D), Porsche 1500; Jacques Herzet/Lucien Bianchi (B), Ferrari 166; Kurt Zeller/Hans Wencher (D), Porsche 1500; Ian Appleyard/Mrs Pat Appleyard (GB), Jaguar XK 120; Baron & Baroness Alex von Falkenhausen (D), Frazer Nash; Herr & Frau Hans Leo von Hoesch (D), Porsche 1500; Ferdinando Gatta/Cottino (I), Lancia B20 2500; Count Johnny Lurani/di Sambuy (I), Lancia B20 2500; Charles Fraikin/Olivier Gendebien (B), Jaguar XK 120; Raymond Stempert/Georges Schwartz (F), Panhard 750; Francisco Bultó-Marqués/J M Llobet (E), Porsche 1500; Salvador Fabregas-Bas/C Apezteguia (E), Lancia B20 2500; Stirling Moss/John Cutts (GB), Sunbeam Alpine; Marcel Schwob d'Héricourt/A de Roquefort (F), Panhard 850; de Caralt/Blesa (E), Porsche 1500; M & Mme Chieusse (F), Panhard 850; George Murray-Frame/John Pearman (GB), Sunbeam Alpine; Paul Persoglio/Gatinel (F), Renault 4CV; John Fitch/Peter Miller US/GB), Sunbeam Alpine; M Poletti/Cipriani (F), Simca; Mr & Mrs Reg Mansbridge (GB), Jaguar XK 120; Asso/Giuseppe Borelly (F/I), Alfa Romeo 1900; Miss Sheila van Damm/ Mrs Anne Hall (GB), Sunbeam Alpine; Marion/Champel (F), Citroën 11 légère.

1954 (11): Wolfgang Denzel/Hubert Stroinigg (A), Denzel; Jean Rédélé/Louis Pons (F), Renault 4CV; Yves Lesur/Maurice Foulgoc (F), Renault 4CV; Henry O'Hara Moore/John Gott (GB), Frazer Nash; Paul Guiraud/Henri Beau (F), Peugeot 203; Maurice Gatsonides/Rob Slotemaker (NL), Triumph TR2; Bill Burton/Burke (GB), Aston Martin; Heinz Meier/Hermann Luba (D), DKW 3-6; Roger Rauch/ Bousson (F), Salmson 2300; Stirling Moss/John Cutts (GB), Sunbeam Alpine; Paul Barbier/Robert Rastit (F), Peugeot 203.

Coupe d'Or: Stirling Moss (GB), Sunbeam-Talbot.

1955: Cancelled

1956 (17): Michel Collange/Huguet (F), Alfa Romeo Giulietta Sprint; Claude Storez/Robert Buchet (F), Porsche; Chuck Wayne/DD Kriplen (US), Porsche; André Blanchard/ Guy Jouanneaux (F), Denzel; Jean-Pierre Estager/Jean Pebrel (F), Ferrari; Paul Ernst Strähle/Hans Wencher (D), Porsche; Cuth Harrison/Edward Harrison (GB), Ford Zephyr; Maurice Gatsonides/Ed Pennybacker (NL), Triumph TR3; Marcel Lauga/François Lauga (F), Denzel; P David/J. Metin (F), Peugeot; Count Charles de Salis/Capt McGregor (GB), Aston Martin; Denis Scott/S Asbury (GB), Ford; Paddy Hopkirk/Willy Cave (EIR/GB), Triumph TR3; Hans & Philip Kat (NL), Triumph TR3; Mrs Nancy Mitchell/Miss Pat Faichney (GB), MG; L Griffiths/T Norman Blockley (GB), Triumph TR3; Tommy Wisdom/Miss Ann Wisdom (GB), Triumph TR3.

Coupe d'Argent: Maurice Gatsonides (NL), Jaguar & Triumph.

1957: Cancelled

1958 (7): Bernard Consten/Roger de Lageneste (F), Alfa Romeo Giulietta SV; Guy Clarou/Pierre Gelé (F), Alfa Romeo Giulietta Berlina; Max Riess/Hans Wencher (D), Alfa Romeo Giulietta Berlina; Keith Ballisat/Alain Bertaut (GB/F), Triumph TR3; Edward Harrison/BPR Haberson (GB), Ford Zephyr; Peter Harper/Peter Jopp (GB), Sunbeam Rapier; William Shepherd/John Williamson (GB), Austin-Healey 100.

1959 (9): Paul Condriller/Georges Robin (F), Renault Dauphine; Hermann Kühne/Hans Wencher (D), Auto-Union/DKW; Paddy Hopkirk/Jack Scott (EIR/GB), Sunbeam Rapier; Jacques Rey/André Guilhaudin (F), DB-Panhard; Peter Riley/Alec Pitts (GB), Ford Zephyr; Peter Jopp/Les Leston (GB), Sunbeam Rapier; Cuth Harrison/John Harrison (GB), Ford Zephyr; Edward Harrison/J William Fleetwood (GB), Ford Zephyr; I 'Tiny' Lewis/Tony Nash (GB), Triumph Herald.

1960 (6): Roger de Lageneste/Henri Gréder (F), Alfa Romeo Giulietta SS; Miss Pat Moss/Miss Ann Wisdom (GB), Austin-Healey 3000; José Behra/René Richard (F), Jaguar 3.8; Eugen Böhringer/Hermann Socher (D), Mercedes 220SE; G 'Bobby' Parkes/G Howarth (GB), Jaguar 3.8; René Trautmann/Jean Claude Ogier (F), Citroën ID 19.

1961 (1): Donald Morley/Erle Morley (GB), Austin Healey 3000.

1962 (5): Donald Morley/Erle Morley (GB), Austin-Healey 3000; Hans Joachim Walter/Kurt Schoettler (D), Porsche Carrera; Miss Pat Moss/ Mrs Pauline Mayman (GB), Austin-Healey; Mike Sutcliffe/Roy Fidler (GB), Triumph TR4; René Trautmann/Patrick Chopin (F), Citroen DS 19.

1963 (6): Jean Rolland/Gabriel Augias (F), Alfa Romeo Giulietta; Rauno Aaltonen/Tony Ambrose (SF/GB), Morris Mini Cooper S; Henry Taylor/ Brian Melia (GB), Ford Cortina GT; David Seigle-Morris/Barry Hercock (GB), Ford Cortina GT; René Trautmann/Yves Cherel (F), Citroen DS 19; Mrs Pauline Mayman/Miss Valerie Domleo (GB), Morris Mini Cooper.

	Coupe d'Argent: René Trautmann (F), Citroën.
1964 (7):	Jean Rolland/Gabriel Augias (F), Alfa Romeo; Vic Elford/David Stone (GB), Ford; Donald Morley/Erle Morley (GB), Austin-Healey; Rauno Aaltonen/Tony Ambrose (GB), Mini Cooper; Jacques Rey/Jean Pierre Hanrioud (F), Porsche; Erik Carlsson/Gunnar Palm (S), Saab; John Wadsworth/Peter Cooke (GB), Mini Cooper.
	Coupe d'Argent: Donald Morley (GB), Austin-Healey.
1965 (8):	René Trautmann/Mlle Claudine Bouchet (F), Lancia; Timo Mäkinen/Paul Easter (SF/GB), Mini Cooper; Henry Taylor/Brian Melia (GB), Ford; Paddy Hopkirk/Henry Liddon (EIR/GB), Mini Cooper; Jean-François Piot/Jean-François Jacob (F), Renault Gordini; Jean Vinatier/H Melot (F), Renault Gordini; Jean Claude Ogier/B Ogier (F), Citroën; Tony Fall/Mike Wood (GB), Mini Cooper.
	Coupe d'Argent: Paddy Hopkirk (EIR), Triumph, Sunbeam & Mini-Cooper.
1966 (7):	Jean Rolland/Gabriel Augias (F), Alfa Romeo; Roger Clark/Brian Melia (GB), Ford; Jean-François Piot/Jean-François Jacob (F), Renault; Henri Gréder/Gilbert Staepelaere (F/B), Ford; Noël Labaune/Paul Etienne (F), Alfa Romeo; Lucien Bianchi/Christian Delferrier (B/F), Citroën; Jean Pierre Nicolas/Claude Roure (F), Renault.
	Coupe d'Argent: Jean Rolland (F), Alfa Romeo.
1967 (4[3]):	Paddy Hopkirk/Ron Crellin (EIR/GB), Mini Cooper; Bernard Consten/Jean-Claude Peray (F), Alfa Romeo; Jean-Claude Gamet/Michel Gamet (F), Alfa Romeo, Harry Källström/Gunnar Häggbom (S), Renault Gordini.
1968 (3):	Jean Vinatier/Jean-François Jacob (F), Renault Alpine; Jean-Louis Barailler/Philippe Fayel (F), Alfa GTA; René Trautmann/Mme Claudine Trautmann (F), Lancia Fulvia HF.
1969 (6):	Jean Vinatier/Jean-François Jacob (F), Renault Alpine; Jean-Claude Andruet/Patrice Ecot (F), Renault Alpine; Jorma Lusenius (S)/Seppo Halme (SF), Renault Alpine; René Trautmann/Mme Claudine Trautmann (F), Lancia Fulvia HF; Harry Källström/Gunnar Häggbom (S), Lancia Fulvia HF; Jean Pierre Nicolas/Claude Roure (F), Renault Alpine.
1970:	Cancelled
1971 (2):	Bernard Darniche/Alain Mahé (F), Renault Alpine; Jean Vinatier/Mlle Lucette Pointet (F), Renault Alpine.
	Coupe d'Or: Jean Vinatier, Renault Alpine.

A total of 166 Coupes des Alpes plus three Coupes d'Or and five Coupes d'Argent were awarded between 1938 and 1971.

ÖSTERREICHISCHE ALPENFAHRT 1949 – 1973
Österreichischer Automobil-, Motorrad- und Touring Club
European Rally Championship events in 1960, 1964, and 1966 to 1972. In 1973 Rally World Championship event.

N° Year/date	Start &. finish	Distance	Starters	Classified	Not penalized	All Alpine Cup winners [4]	1st, General Classification
1949 27/28Aug	Zell am See	1056km	48	17	not applicable	Max Lindner (CH), Simca (T 1100); Karel Vrdlovec (CS), Tatraplan, (T 2000); Ludwig Breit (A), Steyr 220 (T over 2000); Wolfgang Denzel (A), VW-WD Equipment (S 1100); Georg Fallenegger (A), BMW 327/28 (S 2000).	
1950 24/25 June	Velden	1273km	56	35	not applicable	Max Lindner (CH), Simca (T 1100); Karl Hirsch (A), Lancia Aprilia (T 1500); Herbert Günther (A), Chevrolet (T over 2000); Otto Mathé (A), VW-Porsche type 64 (S 1100); Georg Fallenegger (A), BMW 327/28 (S 2000).	
1951 16/17 June	Kitzbühel	1375km	111	58	not applicable	Alois Kopecný CS), Tatraplan [T]; Helm Glöckler (D), Renault 4CV [S].	

Alpine Trials and Rallies 1910 - 1973

N° Year/date	Start &. finish	Distance	Starters	Classified	Not penalized	All Alpine Cup winners [4]	1st, General Classification
1952 21/22 June	Velden	1065km	75	52	38	Karl Hirsch (A), Lancia Aprilia [T]; Dr Siegfried von Pachernegg (A), Denzel 1100 [S].	
1953 19/21 June	Gmunden	1573km	48	29	14	Lothar Stiglechner (A), Steyr-Fiat 1100 [T]; Paul Stegelmann (D), VW 1100 [S].	
1954 10/13 June	Velden	1488km	53	37	5	Wolfgang Denzel (A), Denzel 1300 [S].	
1955 16/19 June	Velden	1460km	50	31	2	0	
1956 15/17 June	Mariazell	1482km	47	25	10	Walter Schatz (A), DKW [T]; Wolfgang Denzel (A), BMW 502 [S]	
1957 13/16 June	BadAussee	1497km	48	41	33	Dr Arnulf Pilhatsch (A), BMW 502 [T]; Hans Bauer (A/I), Alfa Romeo Giulietta Sprint [GT].	
1958 6/8 June	Velden	1699km	71	54	35	Georg Kaufmann (A), Alfa Giulietta TI [T].	
1959 11/14 June	Velden	1699km	63	46	35	Baron Alex von Falkenhausen (D), BMW 600 [T]; Walter Huber (A), Porsche 1300 [GT]; Dr Arnulf Pilhatsch (A), VW-Denzel [S].	
1960 26/29 May	Velden	1680km	75	56	39	Franz Prach (A), Steyr-Puch 500 [T] Dr Arnulf Pilhatsch (A), BMW 700 [GT]	
1961 1/4 June	Velden	1591km	93	66	45	Johannes Ortner (A), Steyr-Puch 500 [T] Rudolf Trefz (D), Porsche Carrera [GT] Dr Arnulf Pilhatsch (A), BMW 700 [S]	
1962 31May/3Jun	Velden	1180km	88	65	33	Johannes Ortner (A), Steyr-Puch 500 [T] Gert Greil (A), Porsche Carrera [GT]	
1963 23/25 May	Velden	1245km	93	43	25	Ferdinand Mitterbauer (A), NSU 600 [T] Wilfried Gass (D), Porsche Carrera [GT] Eduard Wieser (A), DKW [S]	
1964 28/30 May	Velden	1539km	85	65	59	Paddy Hopkirk/Henry Liddon (EIR/GB), Austin-Healey [GT] Arnaldo Cavallari/Rubieri (I), Alfa Romeo Giulia [T]	1st
36th 1965 27/30 May	Velden	1512km	78	45	6	Dr Arnulf Pilhatsch/ Peter Lederer (A), BMW 1800 [T] Johannes Ortner/Karl-Heinz Panowitz (A/D), Steyr-Puch 650 [GT]	1st
37th 1966 12/15 May	Velden	1664km	79	37	3	Paddy Hopkirk/Ron Crellin (EIR/GB), BMC Cooper S [T] Günther Wallrabenstein/Ernst Otto Müller (D), Porsche 911 [GT]	1st
38th 1967 9/13 May	Velden	1738km	66	31	11	Sobiesław Zasada/Jerzy Dobrzanski (PL), Porsche 911 S [GT] Lasse Jönsson/Lasse Ericsson (S), Saab V4 [T]	1st
39th 1968 15/19 May	Semmering	1914km	70	32	14	Bengt Söderström/Gunnar Palm (S), Ford Escort TC [T] Otto Karger/Dr P Wessely (A), Matra Djet 6 [GT]	1st

N° Year/date	Start &. finish	Distance	Starters	Classified	Not penalized	All Alpine Cup winners [4]	1st, General Classification
40th 1969 14/18 May	Semmering	2072km	65	18	7	Hannu Mikkola/Mike Wood (SF/GB), Ford Escort TC [T] Sobiesław Zasada/Zenon Leszczuk (PL), Porsche 911 [GT]	1st
41st 1970 6/10 May	Mönich-kirchen	2251km	54	20	5	Björn Waldegaard/Lars Nyström (S), Porsche 911 [GT] Hakan Lindberg/Sölve Andreasson (S), Saab V4 [SplT] Richard Bochnicek/Sepp Kernmayer (A), Citroën DS 21 [ST]	1st
42nd 1971 12/15 May	Baden	2413km	54	15	0	Ove Andersson/Arne Hertz (S), Renault Alpine [GT] Klaus Russling/Franz Mikes (A), VW 1302S [SplT] Walter Pöltinger/Hans Hartinger, A, BMW 2002 [ST]	1st
43rd 1972 6/9 Sept	Baden	2463km	58	8	2	Hakan Lindberg/Helmut Eisendle (S/I), Fiat 124 Spider [GT] Günther Janger/Harald Gottlieb (A), VW [SplT] Vic Dietmayer/Oswald Schurek (A), A, BMW 2002 [ST]	1st
44th 1973 12/16 Sept	Baden	2265km	74	25	10	Achim Warmbold/Jean Todt (D/F), BMW 2002 [SplT] Bernard Darniche/Alain Mahé (F), Renault Alpine [GT] Vic Dietmayer/W Viakowsky (A), BMW 2002 [ST]	1st

Abbreviations: [GT] = Grand Touring Cars; [S] = Sports Cars; [SplT] = Special Touring Cars; [ST] = Standard Touring Cars; [T] = Touring Cars

JUGOSLOVANSKA ALPSKA VOŽNJA 1952-1955
Auto Moto Zveza Slovenije, start & finish in Bled

Year/date	Overall winner
1952 7 Sept	Alfred Bolz (Saar), Peugeot 203
1953 6 Sept	Alex von Falkenhausen (D), BMW 328
1954 5 Sept	Wolfgang Denzel (A), Denzel 1300
1955 4 Sept	Dušan Maleric (YU), Porsche 1300

Alpine Trials and Rallies 1910 - 1973

COPPA DELLE ALPI 1921-1925
Automobile Club di Milano, Start & Finish Milano

Year/date	Distance	Starters	Classified	Overall winner & Coppa delle Alpi
1921, 7/15 Aug	2306km	25	8	Claudio Sandonnino (I) Itala
1922, 6/16 Aug	2770km	37	13	Pietro Cattaneo (I), Ceirano
1923, 5/15 Aug	2940km	44	25	Ferdinando Minoia (I), OM 469 (1469 cc)
1924, 9/17 Aug	2830km	20	9	Vincenzo Coffani (I), OM
1925, 8/15 Aug	2962km	24	15	Filippo Tassara (I), Bugatti 1500

STELLA ALPINA 1947-1955
Automobile Club Trento, Start & Finish in Trento

Year	Distance	Overall winner
1947	1165km	Piero Taruffi (I), Lancia Aprilia
1948	1420km	Giuseppe 'Nuccio' Bertone (I), Fiat Stanguellini 1100
1949	1481km	Francesco Simontacchi (I), Fiat Stanguellini 1100 S
1950	1196km	Salvatore Ammendola (I), Alfa Romeo 2500
1951	1245km	Salvatore Ammendola (I), Ferrari 195 Inter Coupé
1952	1227km	Ovidio Capelli (I), Fiat 8V GT
1953	1227km	Salvatore Ammendola (I), Lancia Aurelia B20 GT 2500
1954	1060km	Giuseppe Crespi (I), Alfa Romeo 1900 SS
1955	1129km	Olivier Gendebien/Mlle Gilberte Thirion (B), Mercedes 300 SL

Footnotes
[1] A sprint event organized by AC Udine till 1975 and again in 1978; then resurrected in 1987 by Scuderia Friuli.
[2] All rallies started in Marseilles with the exception of 1938/39 (Aix-les-Bains) and 1946 (Annecy).
[3] Beginning with 1967 regulations permitted Alpine Cups despite penalty points on condition that total time in the special stages did not exceed the overall winner's performance by more than 2%. Källström was the first driver to win a Coupe des Alpes despite 2 penalty points.
[4] 1949 and 1950, Alpine Cups were awarded to all class winners. Since 1951 only category winners received Alpine Cups.

Index

Persons and cars shown in the illustrations. Nationality also indicated.

Alpine Trials and Rallies 1910 - 1973

Also in this series –

Each of these books takes the reader on a trip to visit or revisit some aspect of daily life that has now disappeared forever. Evocative period images and entertaining but informed text will take you on a delightful journey backward in time. Pure nostalgia!